Diversity, Identity, and Linkages

Diversity, Identity, and Linkages
Explorations in Historical Ethnography

K.S. SINGH

OXFORD
UNIVERSITY PRESS

OXFORD
UNIVERSITY PRESS

Oxford University Press is a department of the University of Oxford.
It furthers the University's objective of excellence in research, scholarship,
and education by publishing worldwide. Oxford is a registered trademark of
Oxford University Press in the UK and in certain other countries

Published in India by
Oxford University Press
YMCA Library Building, 1, Jai Singh Road, New Delhi 110 001, India

ISBN-13: 978-0-19-807513-4
ISBN-10: 0-19-807513-8

Typeset in 10/13.4 Sabon LT Std
By Excellent Laser Typesetter, Pitampura, Delhi 110 034
Printed in India at G.H. Prints Pvt. Ltd, New Delhi 110 020

Contents

Foreword

I am glad that this set of essays, encapsulating K. Suresh Singh's mature reflections on his lifetime's experience in scholarly explorations, is being presented before the readers. It is perhaps the last and the best of the fruits of a life that was distinguished by an unusual boldness in crossing the boundaries between the world of administrators and scholars, the ethnic and cultural boundaries in this vast country of ours, and the conventional boundaries between the social science disciplines.

The historians' mode of looking at human society is diachronic, while the anthropologists prefer a synchronic approach. However, in the following pages the author opens up a passage between the two. In fact K.S. Singh travelled along the path he outlines here in course of his own life. With his initial training as a historian he started with a perspicacious study of the history of tribal consciousness and political mobilization in *The Dust Storm and the Hanging Mist*. And towards the end of his life his focus, as the Director General of the Anthropological Survey of India, was on ethnography. The path he travelled also meant a huge transition from micro-level research to organized collective research of the macro-level. It is given to very few to be at the head of a vast enterprise of the kind he led. That kind of macro-level exploration of Indian society was not attempted since the days of H.H. Risley, Denzil Ibbetson, W. Crooke, E. Thurston, R.V. Russell, and others in the colonial period. The outcome of the first survey of that scale in post-Independence India was the People of India series volumes. Even though amendments and additions will no doubt be made through later scholarly work, that general and comprehensive survey will remain a lasting memorial to its architect.

I am glad that the few words I write by way of introducing this volume provides me an opportunity to pay my tribute to a friend I admired. I recall how, struggling against adversity and a debilitating infirmity in his last days, Suresh Singh soldiered on to complete his project as a National Fellow of the Indian Council of Historical Research. He also completed a few other unfinished projects. In the present volume we have a collection of essays he published in his last few years. These essays, scattered in various scholarly journals and collections of essays edited by others, were difficult to access. The present book not only serves to conveniently bring them all together, but also to help readers to identify the thrust of the underlying argument connecting different essays.

I think one can group the essays in this volume in terms of three major themes. In the first four essays we look at the indigenous tradition of ethnography as well as the ethnography of indigenous traditions. The texts examined are the Mahabharata, Manu's *Dharmashastra*, and a fourteenth-century scholar Jyotirishwara Thakur's *Varna Ratnakar* which Suniti Kumar Chatterjee regarded as the oldest work in Maithili literature. These texts reveal how an ethnic universe was constructed in Indian tradition. The second group of essays are concerned with colonial ethnography. In these three essays Suresh Singh looks back upon the explorations in the complex of tribes and castes and races which to the colonial ethnographers were like boxes into which they could place different fragments of the whole, the Indian people. His comments on the Census of India and the Anthropological Survey of India are of particular interest since he was in a sense the inheritor of that tradition and also one who broke away from that tradition. One of those who thus broke away was Nirmal Kumar Bose, one of the predecessors of Suresh Singh at the head of the Anthropological Survey of India. In these pages, presumably by accident, Bose is not mentioned; his projects on the All India Anthropological Survey of

Populations and All India Survey of Material Culture anticipated in some ways the People of India project ably led by K.S. Singh. The last four essays constitute the third group, focusing on the nationalist and post-Independence perspective on ethnography. In the essays collected in the last few pages of this volume he addresses the theme of 'unity in diversity', a major theme in the nationalist approach to Indian history. In his emphasis on 'diversities and affinities', on 'pluralism and synthesis', on the concept of 'composite culture', Suresh Singh reveals the fundamental values which inspired his life and work.

SABYASACHI BHATTACHARYA
Former Chairman, Indian Council of Historical Research

Preface

When the People of India (PoI) project was designed in 1984–5, a distinguished historian advised us to keep history out of it as much of the history of people was speculative and the imperative need was to report the existential reality. When the project was completed in 1993, another distinguished historian suggested that history should be brought back and the main findings of the PoI project should be historically explored, and as chairman of the Indian Council of Historical Research he offered on his own a national fellowship. Although I took four years to take it up, I started writing on historical dimensions according to the project. I visited the India Office Library in London to look up the records of the ethnographic survey. Most of the material presented in this report have been published before but are now being put together for the first time.

The PoI project sought to explore diversities of all kinds—biological, ecological, linguistic, and ethnic—and affinities among the communities of India. The project dealt with evolution of identities, territorial and ethnic, multiple identities of communities related to ecology, language, and culture, the relationship of identities, and the impact on the communities of change and development. Emergence of identities, territorial and ethnic, is shaped by ecology and culture in history. The Mahabharata, the first ethnography of India, and

Manu's *Dharmashastra*, the first lexicographical work, are the most comprehensive and time-tested in the current ethnographic scenario. Like all major civilizations India had an ethnic universe of its own that was constructed by scholars and rulers, travellers, and geographers. The bare listing of hills, rivers, and peoples in lexicographical works, and short description of communities occurring in the epics and the Puranas constitute the indigenous tradition. Modern ethnography had its roots in the need for information about people by the colonial government for good governance and for the benefit of British capital. The nationalists responded by building up the paradigm of composite culture of all people of India which was the foundation of the freedom struggle and of the nation state that emerged out of it. The post-colonial ethnography explores diversities and affinities, and addresses all identities equally under the rubric of unity in diversities and diversities in unity, which is not a mantra to be chanted ritually and mechanically but to be observed and absorbed in day-to-day life.

K.S. SINGH

Publisher's Acknowledgements

The publisher acknowledges the following for permission to include the articles in this volume.

India International Centre for 'Ecology, Identity, and Culture', published in Geeti Sen and Ashis Banerjee (eds), *The Human Landscape*, Orient Longman and India International Centre, 2001.

Indian Institute of Advanced Study for 'Ethnography of the Mahabharata'. It was first published as 'Ethnography of the Mahabharata and the North-East', in Ajay Mitra Shastri (ed.), *Mahabharata: The End of an Era (Yuganta)*, Indian Institute of Advanced Study and Aryan Books International, New Delhi, 2004.

Munshiram Manoharlal for 'Manu and Contemporary Indian Ethnography' published in D.N. Jha (ed.), *Society and Ideology in India: Essays in Honour of Professor R.S. Sharma*, Munishiram Manoharlal, New Delhi, 1995.

Manohar for 'The Indigenous Tradition: *Varna Ratnakar* and its Ethnography', published in Hetukar Jha (ed.), *Perspective on Indian Society and History: A Critique*, Manohar, New Delhi, 2002.

Seminar Publications for 'The Anthropological Survey of India: A Historical Perspective', published as 'A Perspective on the ASI' in *Seminar*, no. 495, November 2000. Copyright Seminar Publications.

Abbreviations

ASI	Anthropological Survey of India
CoI	*Census of India*
PoI	People of India
VR	*Varna Ratnakar*

1

Ecology, Identity, and Culture*

IDENTITY THROUGH TERRITORY AND ECOLOGY

The notion of space (*kshetra*) in post-modern anthropology is grounded in objective realities; there is also a subjective dimension to this, in-fluenced inter alia by perceptions of the self and the other. The Greeks identified us by the river Sindhu which they called the Indus; and the Persians identified us by the same river as Hind, Hindu, or Hindusthan. The Sumerians, too, had a word for us, Meluha or Dilamun, probably referring to the north-western part of the subcontinent. This exogenous perception emerged earlier; the internal perception came later.

By the third century BC the Indian subcontinent (including parts of Central Asia) was known as Jambudvipa in Asoka's Minor Rock Edict I of circa 260 BC. The name Jambudvipa was derived from the mythical and mighty Jambu tree (rosewood) which stood at the foot of Mount Meru, and it is described as follows: 'Its trunk is 15 yojanas in girth, its outstanding branches 50 yojanas in length and its height and the extents of its shade 100 yojanas each' (Sircar, 1967: 41). Yet the tree

---

* First published in Geeti Sen and Ashis Banerjee (eds), 2001, *The Human Landscape*, New Delhi: Orient Longman and India International Centre.

is not mythical. It abounds in the land, being described as a wonder tree by ancient environmentalists, as possessed of many attributes and properties, including one of divining underground water streams.

The notion of Jambudvipa gradually expanded to cover the entire universe, divided into islands (*dvipa*) in concentric circles separated by oceans, as known at that time; and Bharat became a part of it.

The name Bharat was derived from a lineage, a people, and was first applied to a part of northern India or rather a large part of it, as suggested in the Hathigumpha inscription of the first century BC, commemorating the victories of Kharvela. By the fifth century AD Bharat had become the name for the subcontinent, bounded by the Himalayas in the north and the two oceans in the south. This description of the subcontinent echoes through writings and poetic compositions: from Kalidasa who glorifies the Himalayas as the king of mountains (*nagadhiraja*) to Rabindranath Tagore and Subramanya Bharti. In 'Sareh jahan se accha' Muhammad Iqbal speaks of the mountain that is the highest standing under the canopy of the sky, a sentinel and a passage.

This 'space' that is India is greatly enriched, as mentioned in ancient and medieval texts, by its expanse of mountains, rivers, forests, pasture lands, deserts, and seacoasts. All these specificities of topography bore highly evocative names which suggest the symbiotic relation between them and the people. Lexicographic works from the Mahabharata to the *Varna Ratnakar*, a Mithila classic of the sixteenth century (K.S. Singh, 1997b), and also Mughal texts like the *Ain-i-Akbari* contain descriptions of these features of ecology.

These aspects of the environment evoked the deepest feeling among the people, as suggested by the rapturous descriptions in the texts. The Mahabharata (Mishra, 1987) speaks of Jambudvipa as the beloved of the gods who wish be born there. In the non-Sanskritic traditions, tribal land everywhere is perceived as bewitchingly green. The Koitur or Gonds in Abujhmarh describe their home as the land of colourful abundance (*shringarvalur dvipa*). In their folksongs, the Mundas describe their land as glittering like gold and shining like silver. While mountains bear Sanskritic names, hills and hillocks still retain their tribal/local names.

Rivers have penetrated deep into the Indian psyche. The Mahabharata describes them with evocative Sanskrit names. There are non-Sanskrit words also for the river—for example, Tajna in the Munda area is known as 'Karkari' in its lower reaches, a river that flows with a pleasant sound. Muhammad Iqbal evokes the imagery of hundreds of rivers playing about in the lap of the land. With the spread of Sanskrit culture, the Ganga became the pre-eminent river of India—a symbol of a pan-India political and cultural identity.

The peninsular kingdom of the Chalukyas and the Rashtrakutas claimed to have brought the river Ganga down to their kingdoms. The Chola king, Rajendra Chola, sent his army to the north and to the Ganga in a symbolic act to relate to the river. The Chola rulers transported vessels of sacred Ganga water to their capital at Tanjore. The Muslim rulers including Muhammad bin Tughluq and Aurangzeb transported water from the Ganga to the Deccan because they considered it good for the health. This 'state of mind' on the Ganga seems to have partly inspired the distinguished engineer/politician K.L. Rao's vision of the Ganga, linking up the northern with the southern rivers, in the current Telugu Ganga project.

The forest is extensively mentioned as *jangala, aatvika, mahakaantara,* and *jharkand* in the Sanskrit and Persian texts (K.S. Singh, 2000c), with corresponding words in various *bhasa*s, including tribal dialects. Two distinct ecological regions, heavily forested and peopled by the communities which are called tribal today, emerged as political regions in the medieval period. They were Jharkhand and Gondwana or Garha, with political economies of their own. They had their own mode of paying tribute in elephants and diamonds, and so on.

The fauna and flora of particular ecological regions lend identity to the land, particularly in tribal areas, to this day. The wild buffalo has a large number of historical names associated with it, from Mysore (Mahisakah) in the south to places such as Mahismati and Mahiskarsikah in north–central India. Gaud, which is both a region and a city in Bengal, probably derived from *gaur*, the bison which roamed the terrain as it still does in part of Palamau and the Himalayas. Once native to Burma, it spread across the heavily forested and hilly tracks of eastern, south–eastern, and central–western India and parts of the Himalayas.

The *Naga* (serpent) is closely associated with fertility, protection of crops, and water. Names associated with Nagas (in Tamil, *arya*) are common all over the country. Kashmir derives its name from the Naga scion, Kashyapmuni, and water springs (naga) such as Anantnaga are named after the Nagas. The study of the water-based Naga people in South-east Asia (Jumsai, 1997) has opened up possibilities of further studies on serpent lore. The Naga people in India seem to be spread across not only the water sites but also the low-lying lands (*pataal*), the hills (naga), and the plains, where they include not only people with Naga totems but also all other autochthones.

Sacralization of the land was a historical process that developed gradually, encompassing distant regions. First, a distinction was made between the 'pure land' which consisted at one time of Madhyadesh and, and the not so sacred land where people were described as degraded; penance had to be performed for visiting them. As local traditions were integrated into a cultural synthesis, sacred sites emerged all over the land—particularly in the remote forested and hilly areas. Thus we have the *pitha*s associated with the Shaiva and Tantric traditions, established by the early medieval period. With the advent of Islam the Sufis, particularly of the Chisti order, established their centres. The dargahs got scattered across distant regions, visited by people of all creeds, showing the innate respect for the sacred in the Indian tradition. This sacred geography reinforced the cultural unity of the land.

The political notion of space, defined as *chakravarti kshetra, vasudha,* or *vasundhara,* emerged early in Indian history. Political space was defined territorially as *janapada, varsha, rashtra,* and so on. These lay within the two broad divisions of the country: the Aryavarta comprising north India, and Dakshinapada comprising the land lying south of the Vindhyas. Dravida is a Sanskrit word which applied to the people of the south; even Adi Shankara described himself as a *Dravida shishu*. The Mahabharata probably has the longest list of territories defined by ethnicity and ecology, as will be mentioned later. As many as fifty-six to seventy-five countries (janapadas) are mentioned in the later texts.

The medieval text continue this historical tradition of conceptualizing the relationship between the ecology of regions and their identity. In the Persian language 'Aryavartha' is replaced by 'Hindustan' as a word for north India and also for the whole country. 'Dakhina' replaces the notion of 'Dakshinapada'. Ferishta, the medieval historian of the Deccan, personifies the concept of Hind, claiming that Dakhin is the son of Hind and that Dakhin has three sons: Maratha, Kanahar (Karnataka), and Tilang (Andhra) (Sherwani and Joshi, 1973).

The Mughal compendium of the *Ain-i-Akbari* seems to carry forward the textual description of the ecological feature of the land contained in the Puranas, amplified with personal observations and substantiated with empirical details. It goes further in describing the geographical and ecological diversities, the cultural specificities of regions, and ethnic identities and peculiarities. Jehangir's memoir, the *Tuzuk-i-Jehangiri*, is probably the first personal statement on the biodiversity and cultural variations in the country. The *Varna Ratnakar* provides the Sanskritic dimension to this medieval perception of ecology.

A major feature of the medieval period is the emergence of language regions, encompassing areas of ecological diversities. Tamilaham or 'the land of sweet language Tamil' had emerged very early in history, with *nadu*s or ecological sub-regions as described in the Sangam literature. The ancient land of Tamilaham, which lay between the hills of Venkatam and the tip of Kanyakumari, consisted of five micro eco-zones called *tinai*: the *kurinci* or the hilly backwoods; the *palai* or the parched areas; the *mullai* or the pastoral tracts; the *marutam* or the wetland areas; and the *neital* or the littoral. The hunters and shifting cultivators of the Vetar and Kuravar inhabited the kurinci; the Maravar, or warrior, the palai; the Tayar (Idaiyar), or pastoralists, the mullai; the Ulavar or ploughmen subsisted on the marutam; and the Partavar or fishermen settled along the neital. It is interesting to observe that this Tamil material is probably the first literature on the relationship between ecological diversities and human settlements. Similar material in other major regions of India emerged later.

Amir Khusrau (AD 1253–1325) was intoxicated with love for his new homeland and prided himself as a 'Hindvi', giving ecological reasons for his love of the land. These are its weather, particularly the winter, the verdant and flowering land which blooms all through the year, the roses which are of different hues, the fragrance of flowers, the fresh fruit such as guava, mango and grapes, and cardamoms, pepper, camphor, and the betel leaf.

The medieval period enhanced the horticultural and agricultural resources of the land. In the *Ain-i-Akbari* Abul Fazl offers us a beautiful description:

[W]ith all its magnitude of extent and the mightiness of its empire it is un-equalled in its climate, its raid succession of harvest and the equable tempera-ment of its people. Notwithstanding its vast size, it is cultivated throughout. You cannot accomplish a stage nor indeed travel a kos without meeting with populous towns and flourishing villages, nor without being gladdened by the sight of sweet waters, delightful verdue and enchanting downs. In the autumn and throughout the depth of winter the plains are green and the trees in foli-age. During the rainy season which extends from the close of the Sun's stay in Gemini to his entry into the sign of Virgo, the elasticity of the atmosphere is enough to transport the most inspirited and lend the vigour of youth to old age. Shall I praise the refulgence of its skies or the marvellous fertility of its soil?

(Abul Fazl 1867–77)

In the course of the anti-colonial struggle, many poets including Rabindranath Tagore, Muhammad Iqbal, and Subramanya Bharti created the territorial identity of the nation by using ecological and ethnic symbols fused with deep emotion. Compositions glorifying the land poured out in all major bhasas. To convey the sense of unity, Tagore combined the symbols of the Himalayas, the Vindhyas and the rivers Ganga, Jamuna, and Sindhu, as well as the different ethno-linguistic identities of Punjab, Gujarat, Dravid, Utkal, and Banga. The national and the regional levels of identity co-existed. Tagore also eulogized the regional and ethnic identity in his composition '*Amar Sonar Bangla*', as did other poets in other bhasas. The distinguished Kannada poet, K.V. Puttappa, sang like this in his poem 'Jaya Bharata Jananiya Tanujate':

Oh! Hail!
Mother Karnataka
Daughter of Mother India!
Peace resort of all people attracts the art lovers
Garden for Hindus Christians
Muslims
Parsis
Jains as well
Oh! Hail! Mother Karnataka.

The famous Malayali poet, Vallathol Narayana Menon, said something similar:

The land where we were born
And we are indeed the servants
Of the land of Bharat, renowned in purity ...
Hearing the name of Bharat
Our mind must be filled with pride
And if the name Kerala is heard
Our blood must pulse in our veins.

Post-colonial discourse has sometimes questioned this dominant paradigm of nationalism. As Jawaharlal Nehru said, the diversities which lay dormant during the freedom struggle came to the fore after independence. Today, there is a transition from the notion of unity in diversity to that of diversities in unity, which underlies the greater understanding of the all-round diversities—ecological, biological, cultural, and linguistic—that exist in the country. The People of India project (PoI) explores these differences and also the affinities that have developed among people—spontaneously, naturally, and effortlessly, as part of the civilizational process.

IDENTITY OF PROFESSIONS AND LANGUAGE

In the multi-level identities of the country—its regions, its communities, and its individuals—there is one level of identity which is essentially related to the professions which derive from the different ecological regions.

The Mahabharata (second century BC to second century AD) provides an example of how the communities of India derived their identities from territories and ecology. The territories, known as janapadas, were well established, such as Anga, Banga, Andhra, Kashi, Mithila, Kurupanchala, and so on. By adding the plural '*ah*', the Mahabharata turns these territorial identities into the peoples called *janah*. In fact, the Mahabharata has the largest number of janahs in the ancient texts, 363 out of 700 listed in the literatures covering the ancient period. The point of interest here is that this list consists of peoples. There are a few references to *jati* and occupational groups as well; the number of jatis swelled to sixty-five (jati and *sankirna jati*) and occupational groups to seventy-one in later literatures (K.S. Singh, 1985).

Barring a few territorial names mentioned above, the majority are derived from ecology. Thus we have mountain dwellers such as Arbukaha (of Mount Abu), Haimvatah (of the Himalayas), and Vindhyamulaka (of the Vindhyas). There are peoples living on the banks of rivers such as Kausijakah (of Kosi), Saindhavah (of Sindhu), Sindhu-sauvirah (of Sindhu), and Bhadras (of the Ganga). There are pastoral peoples such as Pasupah and Govindah, and desert dwellers like Marudha/Maradhah. A large number of forest dwellers are mentioned such as the *jangalah* and *dandakah*, apart from people such as the *adirashtra, vanarasyah, nishad, mundah, savarah, kokuratah* (korku), *karusha* (or kurukh), *kollagir* (or Koli), Nishad, and Bhil. The present day ethnic/language/territorial groups may also be identified such as the Utkal, Chola, and Pandya. There are also some interesting groups such as the 'Ekapada' who ran very fast, the 'Lambakarna' or the people with long ears, and the 'Trinetra' or the three-eyed people, mythologized in Greek accounts (Chetan Singh, 2000).

With the development of the economy and the market, and the growing differentiation, janahs gave way to jatis which proliferated. Two things are of interests to us here. First, the jatis were generally engaged in locally available and resource-based occupations; and second, jatis or local institutions were closely related to the ecology through their occupations, language, dialects, and cultures.

The medieval processes accentuated identities at all levels. At one level, the notion of 'Hindu' articulated by Persian and the Persian knowing elite crystallized. The Hindu in the beginning was pitted against the Turk which was an ethnic category; later the Turk was replaced by the Muslim, a religious category. The Central Asian dynasties who established their rule in India emphasized ethnicity, occupation, and place of residence as markers of identity. Thus we have lists of Turk and Mughal lineages and groups. Akbar refers to his conquest of Afghan mountaineers, the swift-careening, desert-dwelling Balucis and other forest dwellers, apart from many rajas and landowners. The medieval texts not only continue with but also develop further the listing and identifications of 'local, indigenous' communities called zamindars. The *Ain-i-Akbari* contains a list of zamindars belonging to various communities, castes, and tribes, mentioning the Gonds, Bhils, and Kolis as the dominant ones in different parts of Akbar's empire. We also have regional listing of jatis for parts of Rajasthan and Gujarat.

Several regional languages (bhasas) emerged from the fourth to the seventeenth centuries, ranging from Kannada in the fourth to Assamese in the sixteenth. These added the dimension of language to the regional formations. The Mughal *subaah*s were well organized administrative units which had also classified regions in terms of languages, as suggested by names such as Gujarat, Bengal, and Punjab. As mentioned by Jehangir, 'the boundary of the country' should be the same as that of language (Chetan Singh, 2000).

The colonial regime took over many of these provinces. Though the three major presidencies were organized for reasons of administrative expediency, the Bengal presidency broke up owing to the lingual and cultural factor. Assam separated in 1872; Bihar in 1912; Orissa from Bihar in 1936. Again in the post-colonial phase, the reorganization of the states was done on linguistic principles. Even so, all major states of India continue to be diverse. The PoI project has generated its documentation according to the eco-cultural regions, ninety-one of them, for studying the people.

The belief that environment determines the character of a people underlies the stereotypes about people and regions, and it is extensively found in literature. We are told by Abul Fazl that because of the climate the region of Agra had people notorious throughout India for their turbulence, courage, and recklessness. Bengal is perceived as another area where the climate induces 'the dust of dissension' among its people (Chetan Singh, 2000). Colonial literature is replete with such material on stereotypes, including terms of abuse that one community has for another. It is only now, with an enhanced knowledge of diversities within a group or communities, that these old stereotypes are gradually losing their popularity.

The colonial period saw a churning of the ethnographic scenario. Through surveys, gazetteers, ethnographic accounts, and censuses, a reasonably complete ethnographic profile of communities emerged of each province in India, which emphasized the local character of most castes and their occupations rooted in local resources.

At the close of the pre-colonial period, all regions of India were becoming multi-lingual, multi-ethnic, multi-religious, or multi-sectarian. A late Purana from Bengal speaks of the presence of many castes; another account mentions the presence of people of various provinces, sects, and religions in this part of the country. This process of multiple formations intensified during the colonial period, with the migration of traders, artisans, peasants, and workers, with the exploitation of resources, and with the establishment of metropolitan centres and cities. The partition of the country set off migration from the north-west and the east who settled all over the country.

A study of the nomenclatures of major regions including states suggests a close relationship with ecology. Thus Kerala is derived from *kera*, the coconut tree; Karanataka from the black soil (*kannaadu*), or highland, or beautiful land (*karunada*), Punjab or Panchanand from the five rivers; Assam from *asam*, the uneven land or low-lying areas; the earlier name of Pragjyotish has been reinterpreted to mean the land of the early sun, which is now captured in the name Arunachal Pradesh; Manipur's original name Kangleipak means dried land. Within the states again various regions are divided ecologically. Thus we have Assam divided into the two ethnographic worlds of the Brahamputra and the Barak Valley; Jammu and Kashmir has three distinct regions defined by ecology, language, and ethnicity; and Gujarat also has three demarcated in almost similar terms. Of the three new states Jharkhand, as mentioned earlier, is an ecological region; Uttaranchal, or more appropriately Uttarakhand, is a well defined historical region; as is Chhattisgarh which comprises mostly medieval Gondwana.

Sometimes, we tend to forget the ethnic origin of our states. Apart from the Tripuris, the Nagas, and the Mizo, the Gurjars have lent their name of Gujarat, Maharattas to Maharashtra and the Od, the earth diggers, to Odra or Orissa. Within each region and its sub-regions there are places with explicit ecological connotations associated with the elements of nature like water, trees, forests, landscape, soil, and so on.

This formulation also applies to the formation of community identity and sub-communities which are associated with ecological features and occupations. Individuals or groups of individuals carry surnames associated with totems or their villages of origin or place of residence. In addition to the ubiquitous presence of the surname Singh/Sinha which is associated with the lion symbolic of power and status, we have a whole range of surnames particularly in Kashmir, Gujarat, and Maharashtra that are associated with totems which include animals, birds, trees, and so on. The region along the Western Ghats have the unique institution of *devak* or tree exogamy which does not permit marriage among groups having a common devak tree.

It is again within the eco-cultural zone—ninety-one as mentioned earlier—that one can find the clustering of communities with their synonyms/segments/surnames and titles, closely related to languages/ dialects (K.S. Singh [ed.], 1996c). Eighty per cent of the communities/ castes of India are located within or outside the state, and only a few are spread over a large part of the country. Indian pluralism is not only a mattter of language and religion. It is also expressed through the formation and clustering of communities in their locales where language, religion, and communities are closely connected (K.S. Singh [ed.], 1993b).

MATERIAL CULTURE RELATED TO ECOLOGY

The bonding between ecology and culture is suggested in many ways. First, the tribal/folk religion as it survives flourishes at the level of the village and other communities. Thus we have the sacred groves of the tribals and the *devakuli*. There are nearly four thousand of them spread all across the country, regarded as the remnants of the primeval forest with its abode of forest spirits and gods. These could still be preserved and developed as the nodal point of biodiversity conservation programmes. Folk gods like Vithoba of western India (originally the god of shepherds, pastoralists, and hunters) is now venerated as one of the incarnations of the almighty god; the cult of the Aiyappa is associated with tigers; snake groves are found in Kerala; mother goddesses in terracotta are spread all over the country, culminating in the gorgeous iconography of the mother goddess cult in Bengal. There are many other examples of vibrant folk traditions rooted in ecological niches.

The life cycle ceremonies (*lokachara*) are specific to each region of India, related to its ecology and culture that celebrate life. Of particular significance is the ceremony celebrating the onset of the reproductive cycle, known by evocative names in different cultural zones of the country.

The relationship of culture to ecology and biodiversity is explained by folklore. The folklore of communities, particularly tribal communities, explained their relationship with the environment consisting of birds and beasts, the relationship between man and woman, between men and men, not only in the period when the world was young but also later when changes shattered the isolation of the primitive world, evoking a new set of responses to emerging realities.

The impact of ecology on material culture, including settlement patterns, house types, dress, and cuisine was studied by the Anthropological Survey of India (ASI) in its examination of material traits (Bose, 1961). An aerial view of India reveals the various types of settlements: the compact settlement, the linear settlements both with triangular and nebular patterns, and, finally, the isolated or dispersed settlements. The densely populated compact nucleated settlement, or the 'honeycomb' settlement, is specific to the fertile plains, while the isolated/dispersed or semi-compact settlement is peculiar to the hills and arid regions. In both, the hamlet is the unit of settlement formed by one group or caste. In tribal areas where untouchability is weak or non-existent, separate settlements of the untouchables are not generally reported. Kerala has a unique type of settlement with its nuclear household standing out in the landscape. Within this there are three types of cottages. Nomadic and some of the tribal people have temporaray encampments with hemispherical huts. In the settled areas of a large part of India, most of the houses have a rectangular ground plan with sloping roofs, or with flat roofs, the latter to be found mostly in the north-western parts. Then there are houses with a circular ground plan and conical roofs, in the tribal belt and arid regions (Bose, 1961).

The survey of material artefacts (1960) suggests that material items of culture seem to function independently of both language and physical types, returning us back to the prehistoric period. Form the point of distribution of material artefacts the country is generally divided into the east and the west, influenced by the culture of South-east Asia and Central and Western Asia. It is presumed that simple methods of pottery manufactured by hand, and one or two special varieties of the plough and yoke, and the portable, multi-socketed wooden mortars for husking paddy came from South-east Asia (Bose, 1961).

These artefacts have been adapted to local resources and skills. For example, basketry is the most widespread of the artefact with both a national spread and regional character in terms of the material used, the techniques, the designs, and the decorations made by various groups within a particular region, depending on its ecological conditions and resource endowments. Bamboo is the most common raw material used for making baskets. Apart from bamboo, other materials used are twig in Jammu and Kashmir, Himachal Pradesh, Maharashtra, and Uttar Pradesh; straw in the Punjab; reed tied with leather string in Rajasthan; grass in Uttar Pradesh; and cane in West Bengal, Assam, and other states of north-east India. Checks, twill and twine are the common techniques used.

The coiling technique is used only in some parts of northern India. Semi-conical and flat-walled baskets are common in both the northern and southern states. Conical baskets are relatively rare. Cylindrical baskets are rare in the eastern states but common in the western ones. Except in Himachal Pradesh and other northern states, baskets with constriction are rare; circular and semi-circular baskets are most widely prevalent across the country (Chetan Singh, 2000).

According to the survey, India is divided into broad zones rather than regions in matters of dress. For example, ecology makes Rajasthan and the arid areas the most colourful zones. Clothing is one of the various devices of adaptation to the ecology marked by the blazing sun and the fierce winds. It also reflects social status and hierarchy unique to the feudal order, and the current levels of aspirations of a people or region.

The diversity of Indian foods and food habits are reflected in their cuisine. Jehangir mentions the food habits of the people of Gujarat, especially the '*khichri* of bajra' which they call '*laziz*'. Food is an aspect of culture shaped by the environment, the availability of resources including staple cereals, pulses, spices, and condiments, and the cooking medium. It is also much influenced by vegetarian and non-vegetarian traditions, gender role in the preparation of food, and access to food. The survey (1960) showed that a major part of the country had its staple diet of wheat flour made into bread, or millet flour boiled whole or made into bread in the north-western and adjoining parts of central India. Rice boiled whole was the dominant staple in eastern and north-eastern India and the western sea coast.

Within this broad division different regions of India have their own cuisine. For example, Rajasthan's cuisine is influenced by concerns for scarcity of water, lack of fuel or heating, and the need to have food that could last several days. Therefore Rajasthani diet involves a minimum use of water during preparation. With its rich cattle wealth, milk and clarified butter, and locally grown beans and indigenous plants are used generously however. Various areas of Rajasthan have their own popular varities of sweets as well. In recent years, knowledge of local foods and access to them have grown phenomenally.

Ecology, identity, and culture are not only interrelated, they are diverse, heterogenous, and complex. Each one of them is a dynamic process in itself and in relation to the other, as processes of change and development as also of interaction. Ecology is only one of the levels of identity along with language, culture, politics, and economy. Yet, it is reassuring to recall, amidst the maelstrom of competing identities and at times conflicting loyalties, one's rootedness in ecology and culture.

2

Ethnography of the Mahabharata*

This chapter seeks to explore the ethnographic dimensions of the Mahabharata in terms of the parameters of the contemporary ethnographic project (1985–2000) on the People of India (PoI). The dimensions include (i) a notion of space, (ii) the emergence of territorial and ethnic identities, (iii) identification, listing, and distribution of people, (iv) the linkages and affinities among people, and (v) the diffusion of the Mahabharata traditions.

The Mahabharata corpus, as it has come down to us, has evolved, absorbed, and incorporated many traditions across the centuries, particularly during the period between the second century BC and the second century AD when it was mainly compiled. As it developed from Jaya to Bharatato Mahabharata, it became the story of the people of all of India. Indeed, the Mahabharata is a great assemblage of peoples, 363 of them, which is the largest number in the ancient texts. They meet on the battlefield as equals—an enemy is not to be underrated—and are generally mentioned in respectful terms, even outside

* First published as 'Ethnography of the Mahabharata and the North-East', in Ajay Mitra Shastri (ed.), 2004, *Mahabharata: The End of an Era (Yuganta)*, New Delhi: Indian Institute of Advanced Study and Aryan Books International.

the battlefield. They are also bound by many ties and have many linkages, which speak of the vitality, maturity, and understanding of a civilization process, reflecting the consciousness of a vibrant civilization.

The second part of this chapter deals with the north-east including the hills, which like other parts of India has its linkages with the epic, its heroes, and its episodes through an ongoing process of creative adaptation. There are four aspects to it. First, the participation of Bhagdatta with his army of Chinas and Kiratas in the Kurukshetra war; second, the Sanskritization of tribes and the reconstruction of genealogies linking them to the Mahabharata characters like Bhima, Hidimba, Ghatotkacha, and Arjuna—their, their legends and folklores about the visit of the Mahabharata heroes and matrimonial alliances; Mahabharata themes that figure prominently in the literature and performing arts (leading some communities to call themselves Mahabharata) and fourth the critical re-examination of some of these reconstructions today as the north-eastern communities engage in a search for identity.

The Mahabharata, probably the first comprehensive ethnography of India, has been explored as such by scholars, particularly historians, who have generally applied the colonial concept of tribe to describe the people (*jana*). While it is not my purpose here to present an overview of the literature in this field, one may briefly mention the leads thrown up by three important pieces of writing. The first is the *Ethnography of Ancient India* by Robert Shafer (1954) which, despite the title, concentrates on the ethnography of the Mahabharata rather than the whole of ancient India. What impresses this author is the 'great number of ethnic names' of 'nations, tribes or regions', about three hundred of them—in fact, it is 363, which is much more than the geographical names given in the Puranas—which he finds 'much more limited and much more corrupt' than the list given in the Mahabharata. He also describes the Mahabharata as an original 'Kuru epic', developed with later compilations and interpolations over several hundred years. He further describes the epic as essentially the story of a native rebellion, led by the Kauravas against the Aryan exploitation symbolized by the Pandavas, who forced 'tribes and nations', particularly the non-Aryans, to pay exorbitant tribute and acknowledge the overlordship of Yudhishthira. The epic, according to him, is thus an apologia for the Pandavas, their eulogy—in fact an apologia for the extermination of Kshatriyas resulting from the Mahabharata war. Such views however are not entirely supported by the reading of the Mahabharata as it exists today. While Aryanization in terms of the spread of the Indo-Aryan language, Sanskrit, was underway, a synthesis of various cultures was emerging, a mixture of morphological types was going on. The native non-Aryan groups fought on both sides, the larger number, no doubt, on the side of the Kauravas because they were in power and had a larger army. The Mahabharata established the primacy of the Pandavas and their mentor, Lord Krishna, for forty years till it was challenged by peoples on the periphery. Such things were going on all the time in Indian history. Robert Shafer has a point when he says that the people speaking Tibeto-Burman languages once occupied the Ganga valley or parts of it, and probably gave us such names as the Ganga. Anga, Vanga, and Kalinga, though today they are confined to the Himalayas and the north-east. However, it is difficult to agree with the view that at the time of the Mahabharata, the Aryans were the invaders and the land was dominated by non-Aryans, or that the waves of Indo-Aryans moved from Kailash–Mansarovar region along the Sutlej to the north-western part of the subcontinent, and from there towards the Ganga–Yamuna valley. Although Aryanization had been going on at a 'geometric rather than arithmetic rate' (Shafer, 1954: 6) for the last 2,000 years, the process was not so complete at the time of the Mahabharata, nor is it so even today. There is a shade of racism in Shafer's analysis when he talks too literally of the gradation of colours for the four *varna*s. Also it is wrong to say that the Vaishyas were Tibeto-Burmans. The identification of 'races' with cultures and languages is not generally accepted today. Shafer quotes Patanjali to describe the Brahmanas as having a white complexion and yellow and red hair; there are also references to Krishna and other dark-skinned Brahmanas of which Veda Vyasa was an example. The PoI study of Brahmana groups shows that they are quite heterogeneous in terms of biological, cultural, and linguistic traits. The Bhils were not Nahals. In fact, the Nahali language is neither Mundari nor Dravidian. Bhili is now accepted as a member of the Indo-Aryan language family.

Certainly the Mahabharata presents a picture of a mixed society with people, particularly rulers, marrying across social groups, speaking different languages and practising different cultures, and of an emerging synthesis, which has been the hallmark of Indian civilization from the beginning.

K.C. Mishra's *Tribes in Mahabharata* is a major work which describes many dimensions of the Mahabharata including its ethnography both at territorial and ethnic levels. Like Shafer, he deals with the various lists of the tribes compiled in the Mahabharata but persists, like other historians, with the colonial notion of the tribe. This work is followed by Mamata Chaudhary's *Tribes of Ancient India* (1951) in which she puts the number of the tribes mentioned in the ancient texts at about 700, almost half of which is mentioned in the Mahabharata. Although she valiantly tries to define the tribe in the traditional anthropological sense, as an 'aggregate of stocks of kindred persons forming a community, claiming descent from a common ancestor' her use of the word 'tribe', as by other historians using this notion from nineteenth century Indian ethnography, is not free from difficulties. In fact, the right course from the historians would have been to use the native Sanskrit term, jana, mentioned in the Mahabharata and other texts.

This is an issue taken up by the distinguished historian Niharranjan Ray (K.S. Singh [ed.], 1972: 6–15). He uses the native terms jana and *jati*, which he rightly says have the same roots, that is, *jan*, that is, to be born into or give birth to. Thus, Ray makes a distinction between *jana*, which he identifies with the communities, peoples, and present-day tribes, and jati, which he describes as a complex production organization. Both have something to do with birth and biological heredity and hence with familial and social relationships. But behaviorally, as seen through history, they also have a social and economic purpose and function, regulated by birth and heredity. Here was thus a system which was directed not towards mobility but towards stability and security.

Ray mentions a whole lot of janas:

[T]he Savaras, the Kulutas, the Kollas, the Bhillas, the Khasas, the Kinnaras and a countless number of many others whom today we know as 'tribes', bearing almost the same recognizable names ... It is significant that in this huge body of literature whenever such and other communities of people find mention, they are always referred to in the plural number, collectively as a people or *janah, Andhrah, Savarah, Kinnarah,* and so on. An analysis of such names and the context in which they are referred to shows very clearly and unmistakably that all such communities had each territorial habitat of their own which can still be identified.

With the passage of time, each of these communities lent their names to the territory inhabited by them, and the territories came to be known as *padas.* Most of the local names of districts, divisions and states that we know of today, have come down to us from the *padas* of old; but quite a number of them have also lost their name and identity in their larger and more powerful neighbours ... (K.S. Singh [ed.], 1972)

A careful analysis of the long list of janas in the epics, and the Buddhist, Puranic, and secular literature of early and medieval times and the context in which they are mentioned, makes it very clear that hardly any distinction was made, until very late in history, between what we know today as 'tribes' and such communities of people who were known as the Gandharas and Kambojas, Kasis and Kosalas, Angas and Magadhas, Kurus and Panchalas, for instance. At any rate, in the whole body of historical data at our disposal, there is hardly anything to suggest that these communities of people belonged to two different social and ethnic categories. In fact, in the literary sources I have referred to, between the communities of people whom today we refer to as 'tribe', and those that we know from history as belonging to more advanced stages of socio-economic and cultural growth, there is hardly any evidence to show that in the collective consciousness of India there is any difference between the two sets of janas.

According to Ray, there are three type of janas—first, those of foreign origin who were absorbed into the brahmanical religion and the socio-economic production system of jati.

One has only to remember what happened to the Sakas, the Kushanas, the Abhiras, the Jnatrikas or Jats, the Gujars, the Huns or Hunas, and other allied peoples, many of whom are mentioned as *janas* in the list of people as given in the epics and the Puranas, in the Buddhist and secular literature and in a land grants and other historical documents. The Islamized Turkas,

Afghans, Iranians and Mongols were certainly able to maintain their religious and cultural identity, even to extend the frontiers of Muslim society within India, but let it be noted that they too had to succumb to the socio-economic organization of Brahmanical Hinduism, to the same production system as that of the *jati*. Indeed, once they had fallen into the production system of the *jati* it was no longer possible for them to resist its social implications. The same thing happened to the communities of people of the Tibeto-Burman stock who trudged into Assam and our north-eastern regions in the thirteenth century. Those of the *janas* of foreign origin that came to exercise political authority as kings and as member of royalty, nobility and the court, were given the *jati* status for Kshatriyas; those that eventually took to agriculture came to be self-styled as Vaisyas; but the larger majority had to be content with very low *jati* status in Hindu socio-economic hierarchy, including those like the Hunas who allowed themselves to be recruited as mercenary soldiers by regional rulers. (K.S. Singh [ed.], 1972)

Second, there were janas of indigenous (this term has become controversial) origin who were absorbed into the Hindu-brahmanical social organization. Those '*janas* who were defeated in war and taken prisoners, were immediately made economically and socially subservient altogether, being reduced to slaves, labourers and servants. Eventually, they came to be incorporated in[to] the Hindu social organization, but seem to have been given a place at the lowest bottom, not very different from that of the *Chandalas*.'

Third, there were janas who were in the periphery of Aryavarta:

These were janas that today lie all along our eastern and north-eastern frontiers and along the central and western Himalayas up to a bright of 13,000 feet, janas that are predominantly of the Tibeto-Burman stock, except perhaps the Nagas and one or two other less[er] known janas. This entire Himalayan area from our eastern frontiers to Ladakh is naturally a very sensitive one, and for more than one reason, a very significant one as well from the political and economic points of view. Many of these janas do not, for obvious reasons, make their appearance in history or in our historical geography before the nineteenth century, but many others do, for instance, the Nagas who are mentioned by Ptolemy in the second century AD, the Khasas, the Kiratas which seem to be almost a blanket name for all the Tibeto-Burman peoples in our eastern and north-eastern frontiers, the Kinnaras of the Kinnaur district of Himachal, the Kullutas of the Kullu valley, the Bhotas of the Bhutan-Sikkim area, and a few others whose names appear in the traditional Puranic list of janas. Our medieval Assamese, Bengali, Maithili and Hindi literature, too, gives us a few names of such peoples.

Then there is a belt of jana territory in middle India and the Islands. Then there is the whole belt along the old Paryiyatra, Vindhya and Suktimat hills which are collectively known to us as the Vindhyan ranges, stretching from almost the borders of Rajasthan to what are called the Chhotanagpur and Orissa hills which are but extensions of the Vindhya ranges. All along these ranges and their slopes and feet and in the forests and valleys nursed by them live and have been living for centuries some of the oldest janas known to our history and culture[,] the Nishadas and the Savaras, the Kollas and Bhilla, for instance, and many other cognate and semi-cognate *janas* of whom history and historical geography have not kept any record. But we know from one of our epic[s], the Ramayana, that part at any rate of this area was the region that was called *janasthana*, the land par excellence of the *janas*. Ethnically the majority of the *janas* seem to be of proto-Austroloid origin though a few of them speak [a] language of Dravidian affiliation.

Besides these two geographical areas of non-*jati* janas there is also a good number of them in smaller aggregates and dispersed in relatively smaller areas in almost all the southern States, especially in Andhra Pradesh and Kerala, and [in] Maharashtra. But these *janas* are all more or less in close contact and communication with socially and culturally, politically and economically more powerful communities belonging to the *jati* complex. And finally there are the isolated aggregates of relatively much less developed *janas* in the Andaman and Nicobar Islands. (K.S. Singh [ed.], 1972)

The PoI project based on an ethnographic survey of all people of India reinforced the view that India is a land of many communities. These communities called janas in the ancient texts are the original formations, the basic units of our civilization, rooted in ecology, in the resource endowments of various regions, and in their social and cultural organizations, their languages and dialects. Even though they have evolved from the simple to the complex social organization or complex systems of production as Niharranjan Ray puts it, they share many traits of a community, such as endogamy, resource-based occupations, notions of purity and pollution, order of hierarchy in incipient or developed forms. From this point of view the tribes are at one end of the pole and the present-day scenario at the other end, but both are people, the jana, the inhabitants of the land. The tribes are the relatively isolated janas, distant and backward. The distinction made by Ray between jana and jati is not supported by the ancient texts (the Mahabharata, as will be described later, treats janas as neither tribe nor caste, but as people) which generally treat them interchangeably, and later mention jatis more than janas which is fact fades away.

II

We now turn to the salient features of the ethnography of the Mahabharata.

The first is the notion of space, which is crucial to ethnography as people at one level of their multi-level identity generally derive their identity from space. In the ancient period there was the notion of *bhumi, vasudha,* or *chakravarti-kshetra,* which was the political space to be conquered and ruled. Jambudvipa was the name given to this space. This name, for the first time, occurs in the Asokan inscriptions. The Mahabharata has a chapter entitled 'Jambudvipanirmana-khanda'—section V of Bhishmaparvan. Jambudvipa derives its identity from the jambu tree which is both mythical as it is believed to stand near Mount Meru, and real because the land abounds in jambu trees. It has been rapturously described by ancient environmentalists as a wonder tree gifted with many attributes and properties. However, the notion of 'Jambudvipa' gradually expanded from its first description which applied to the Asokan empire to mind-boggling proportions as this was gradually extended to include greater India and even beyond that to all continents (except the Americas and Australia). It is said in the Mahabharata and its later versions that there were seven divisions (*varsha*s) of the Jambukhanda (section XI of Bhishmaparvan) including Bharata. Bharatavarsha, located in Jambudvipa, gradually became a part of it (*Jambudvipe Bharatkhande*).

The Mahabharata speaks of the love of the land, and states that the tract of land known by Bharata's name is the beloved land of Manu and Indra. The notion of Bharata is also derived from the founder of the Bharata lineage, which gradually widened to cover the entire country south of the Himalayas and bounded by the oceans. This notion of Bharatavarsha crystallized in the *Vishnu Purana* and came to be celebrated in the literary works composed by Kalidasa, Rabindranath Tagore, and Subramanya Bharti.

This Jambudvipa is criss-crossed by mountains, rivers, forests, deserts, pasture lands, and sea coasts. The name of these mountains and rivers also occurs in many lexicographic works. The six mountains extend from the eastern to the western boundaries including Himavatta, and there are hundreds of rivers with beautiful names of which many can be identified in different parts of the country today.

The land was divided into *janapada*, peopled by specific groups. The relationship between jana and janapada was intimate. Both were interchangeable concepts. The Mahabharata describes the Jambukhanda in mythical terms as a great sect of humanity where men are all of golden complexion and women are like apsaras, and all are without sickness and sorrow and always cheerful. It also notes the bio-ethnic diversity of India where reside people of different jatis (*vaasanti teshu saltvani nanajatini sarvashah, idam tu Bharatam varsham tato haimavatam param*). The space was also traditionally divided into countries (*varsha*s or *rashtra*s). A rashtra is a territorial unit occupied by people, like Adirashtra and Goparashtra.

There was also the notion of sacred land. The core of the culture and religion of the Indo-Aryans was formed by Kuru-Panchala and Matsya land. There were lands which were degraded such as the Sindhu land or the Vahlika where foreigners lived.

The Mahabharata mentions jati occasionally as segments of jana; for example, various jatis of Kiratas are mentioned (*Kiratanam cha jatayah*), or jati and jana seem to be interchangeable terms. There is also a mention of *kula* (*vaisya-sudra kulani cha*). However, most of the names are in terms of jana and janapada. Later texts mention as many as sixty-five jatis and seventy-one occupational groups. Historians are more concerned with jati than jana, and with the transition from varna to jati, the proliferation of the jati, and so on.

As mentioned earlier, the Mahabharata is the most comprehensive ethnography of ancient India in terms of the identification and listing of communities or janas and their territories or janapada. There were 363 of them in all.

The listing of communities in the Mahabharata is based on a number of inventories including 'geography' (231 entries), the *digvijaya* list (212), the *dyuta* or tribute to the Pandavas (296), army formation (158), and additional data (108) as Shafer (1954) puts it. There are a number of repetitions in the list however. The digvijaya campaigns were led by the four Pandava brothers—Bhima in the east, Arjuna in the north, Nakula in the west, and Sahadeva in the south. Karna also was on his digvijaya trail, mostly in the east and also in the north. The list contains a lot of names of the people (jana). A few places are also mentioned, such as Avanti, Kunti, Kuru, Kasi, and so on.

To illustrate our point, we will name some of the communities here. The north-west (Central Asia, Persia, and Afghanistan) was dominated by 'foreigners', namely the Pahlavas, Sakas, Hunas, Yavanas, Kambojas, and Bhlikas. The west, roughly comprising Kashmir, Punjab, Rajasthan, and Gujarat, had communities such as the Daradas (Darda of today), Pisachas, Vahilkas, Yadavas of various segments, Surashtras, and many others. The northern Himalayan region had the Trigartas, Khasas, and others, who were also spread across the plains. The east had the Angas, Vangas, Kiratas, Chinas, and Pundras. The south had the Cholas, Pandyas, Keralas, Andhras, Dravidas, Karnatas, and Mushakas.

Apart from these ethnic categories, there were also communities who derived their identities through ecology. The mountain dwellers included the Arbuadas (Mount Abu), Haimvatas, Vindhyamulakas; from the deserts, the Marudha; from rivers and waterfronts, the Kausijakas (Kosi), Saindhavras (Sindhu), and Sindhu-Sauviras; from the pastures, the Pasupas and Govindas; from the frontier, the Aparants. However, a large number of people belonged to the forests, *jangala*s, *dandaka*s, and so on, because these were abundant in those days. They should be seen together with the forest dwelling communities such as the Adirashtras, Vanarasyas (there is a community called the Vana-manush too), and Nishadas. Some contemporary tribes can be identified as well, like the Mundas, Savaras, Kokuratas or Korkus, Karushas or Kurukhs, Kollagirs or Kolis, and Nishadas or Bhils.

An analysis of this list of communities shows that they were mostly concentrated in the north-western and western parts of the subcontinent and the central region later known as Madhyadesha. The number in the south, the east, and the north-east are few.

When the first encounter of peoples took place in the court of Yudhishthira or on the battlefield, some looked so different, even strange, that they were noted for their style of living or dressing, or plain mythologized as in Greek accounts. There were the Ekapada, that is, the people who ran so fast that it appeared they had only one leg (the author was told about a community among the de-notified groups in western India which fitted this description). There were the Lambakarna, that is, the people with long ears—obviously those who wore turbans with their tails hanging on both sides. And the Trinetra, the three-eyed people, who were probably those who put on a prominent *tattoo* mark or *a tattoo tilaka* shaped like an eye in the middle of their forehead.

The Mahabharata describes some people as low, barbarous, sinful, born of the mythical cow of Vasishtha. But it also contains positive descriptions of the people described as the Mlechhas, such as their martial prowess, their resources including chariots of good quality or horses of good breed, their fertile country, and sometimes their dress and language which was not intelligible. The epic also shows how various communities, who met on the battlefield or outside, had generally developed a mature, healthy, and respectful relationship among themselves, which derived from the sharing of certain values that were common. There were also experiences of living together including studying together—Bhagadatta and Pandu had studied together—abiding friendships, and so on. Some communities had even made attempts to avoid the war. Thus, the Cholas and Pandyas, according to the local version of the Mahabharata, tried to mediate, throwing a feast to which they invited both the Kauravas and the Pandavas, though eventually they sided with the latter.

People are described in clusters such as Kuru–Panchala, and Kasi–Kosala–Karusha. Migrations of peoples are indicated generally not only from the west to the east or from the north to the south (Malwa), but also from the east to the west, particularly those who were driven out by Jarasandha. The power equation among communities was in a state of flux. The Kurus were the dominant group with the Yadavas as a close second. Some communities were in a state of decline such as the Haihaya, Videha, and the Gangas in the north-west. The sheer range of ethnic diversities is fascinating.

The Kiratas or the Indo-Mongoloids need to be specially mentioned here because in recent years there is an effort to distinguish the East Asians from the Central Asians. In the Mahabharata, we can identify the East Asian in terms of the Chinese or the Tibetan-Mongoloids, and the Kiratas. The Nagas of the north-east are mentioned by Ptolemy. Central Asian Mongoloid groups including the Sakas and Hunas, were also known. The Mahabharata gives a graphic description of the Kiratas. They were golden coloured (yellow) tribes whose army looked like a forest of yellow *karnikara* flowers, and they lived on tubers and fruits. They were clad in skin, were strongly built, and wore steel coats of mail. They came from Himavat and seemed from a distance to be of a smoky colour. They had well trained elephants.

The Nagas from elsewhere in the country are not included in the list of janas and janapadas, but some of their branches are mentioned, like the Kokara (identified by the author with Kokrah, that is, modern Chhotanagpur). However, recent researches in history and anthropology of the Nagas persuade us to look afresh at the Naga material in the Mahabharata. They are supposed to have occupied *patala* which was near Hastinapur. But the Nagas as a folk community occupied a much larger and more diversified space including hills, plains, sea-coasts, and so on, having only the Naga totem as their marker. According to the Mahabharata, one branch of Nagas, the Takshakas, occupied the territory from Takshasila up to Hastinapur, and the other branch, the Karkotakas, was distributed from Vindhya to Khukhra which later became the name of medieval Chhotanagpur. The Pandavas had incurred the wrath of Takshaka by burning down the forest for their capital. The Nagas seemed to have supported the Kauravas in the battle even though Kunti was a Naga-*kanya*. In fact, both the Yadavas and Nagas were in close interaction with one another as they settled down as agriculturists. Balarama, who was an incarnation of Seshanaga, had the plough as his weapon. After the Mahabharata war, Arjuna went out on a mission to placate the Nagas, married Ulupi and begot a son, Yeravan. But Takshaka never forgave the Pandavas. The

Nagas had killed the Pandava ancestor, Parikshit, whose son Janamejaya took a terrible revenge by massacring the Nagas and scattering
them far and wide. Many Naga families in middle India trace their
origin to this episode. Janamejaya later married Takshaka's daughter
and peace was restored between the Nagas and the Pandavas.

III

The Mahabharata traditions have become diffused widely. Like all
regions of India and many parts of South-east Asia, the north-eastern
region perceives its linkages with the Mahabharata tradition in a
number of ways. The Mahabharata heroes including Lord Krishna
is believed to have visited some places in this region, and certain
episodes in the epic are associated with their literature, folk tradition,
and performing arts. The Mahabharata heroes also married locally
(K.S. Singh, 1992).

The most explicit reference to the north-east, including the hills,
occurs in the Mahabharata war with reference to the heroic deeds
performed by, and the powerful support given to, the Kauravas by
Bhagadatta, the ruler of Pragjyotisha (the land of the early sun). He
was the son of Naraka, the founder of the dynasty bearing the same
name, who was born of the union of Bhumi (Mother Earth) and a
wild boar. There is a profound symbolism in the original myth bereft
of the brahmanical embellishments that occurred later. The boar was
the most powerful creature of the period, which could move with the
speed of wind and gore to death an elephant or a tiger. It could lift the
earth and was apotheosized into an incarnation of Vishnu. The Earth
was mother to many tribes including the Mundas (*enga* is their word
for mother). Naraka was the founder of the first and the longest sur-
viving dynasty before the Ahoms appeared on the scene. According to
another tradition, Naraka was born at the foot of the hills. He was the
lord of the Kiratas, the Himalayan mountain people, and the Chinas
(the Tibetan-Mongoloids) representing the East Asians, and the kingdom included the north-eastern hills and the low-lying marshy land
south of Assam. Naraka, who had become irreligious and presumptu-
ous and possessed of demoniac ideas, was killed by Krishna. He was

succeeded by his son Bhagadatta. Krishna is also said to have rescued 16,100 women from the custody of Naraka and married them. B.K. Barua (1951) describes Bhagadatta as follows:

Bhagadatta is frequently mentioned in the Mahabharata as [a] powerful warrior. He is celebrated as a 'warrior king' and 'the mighty king of the mlecchas', and is described as 'the best wielder of the elephant goat', among the kings assembled on the Kaurava side in the Great War and as 'skillful with the chariot'. Bhagadatta alone of the northern kings is famed for his long and equal contest with Arjuna. He is dignified with the title 'Siva's friend' esteemed as being not inferior to Sakra in battle. He is also specially named 'the friend of Pandu', and is referred to in terms of respect and kindness by Krishna when addressing Yudhisthira: 'Bhagadatta is thy father's aged friend[,] he was noted for his difference to thy father in word and deed, and he is mentally bound by affection and devoted to thee like a father'. Bhagadatta was killed in the Mahabharata war and was succeeded by his son Vajradatta

(B.K. Barua, 1951: 18–19).

Krishna is said to have again intervened in the affairs in Assam. The Bodos told the author that they had given Krishna his spouse Rukmini who was a Kirata woman of immense beauty. Krishna fell in love with her, and she taught him the art of dancing known as garba which is performed during Navaratra. While the author is not sure of the authority that the Bodos cited for it, this version figures prominently in the local literature as well. In fact, it is celebrated in a work called *Rukmini Harana*. Rukumini's father, Bhishmaka, had his capital at Kundina, a name which survives in the Kundil river at Sadiya.

A somewhat controversial connection with the Mahabharata tradition relates to Manipur. According to an eighteenth-century account, a Manipur ruler, Garib Nawaz (1707–1748), publicly embraced Brahmanism and is said to have replaced the original name of Kanglei (pak), that is, the dry land, with Mekhala (female wrapper worn by Parvati which fell on the land) and Manipur. Shiva drained away the water in the valley through a tunnel which was made by his trident (*trisula*). The serpent god Ananta was so overjoyed that he sprinkled the land with sparkling gems (*mani*). Arjuna is said to have visited Manipur twice. On the first occasion he married the princess

Chitrangada and begot a son named Babhruvahana. Historians, however, are unanimous in rejecting the identification of modern-day Manipur in the Mahabharata, choosing to identify the place in Kalinga along the Mahendra mountains, that is, the Eastern Ghats. However, the Brahmakhanda of the Bhavishya Purana, a work of the fourteenth century, mentions a cluster of kingdoms in the east including Brendra, Tamralipta, Hidimba, Manipurakam, Tripuram, and so on. But this evidence is of doubtful value.

The resurgent Meiteis in their search for identity repudiate the Mahabharata connections (Kabui, 2003). However, the Puranic version continues to be peddled. For instance, in the TV serial titled *Mahabharata ke Baad ki Katha* ('The Story after the Mahabharata') there is a new spin on the Mahabharata connection with Manipur. The mother of Bhishma, Ganga, through her sister Kamakhya, the presiding deity of Assam, conspires to get Arjuna killed by his Kirata son, Babhruvahana, to avenge Bhishma's death at the hands of the Pandava hero! But Krishna's intervention restores the life of Arjuna.

The third intervention by Krishna occurred when he rescued his grandson Aniruddha form the custody of Bana, and got him and Bana's daughter Usha married formally. Tejpur has now been renamed Sonitapur, the capital of Bana, where his fort and the place where Usha and Aniruddha met and secretly married according to Gandharva rites are still identified.

The Sanskritization of tribal chiefs between the seventeenth and eighteenth centuries witnessed the linking of these rulers with the Mahabharata heroes. Bhima was the favourite link through his wife Hidimbi, who is considered a Himalayan spirit (Aryan, 1992), and their son Ghatotkacha is identified with the Kachhari rulers. The capital of the Kachhari kingdom, Dimapur, is a corruption of Hidimbapur. In fact, Hidimba was the old name of Kachhar. According to Endle (1911), the Kachhari ruler Krishna Chandra and his brother Govinda Chandra were both placed inside the body of a large copper image of a now reminiscent of *hiranyagarbha* ritual for purification, and accepted Bhima as their mythological ancestor. The Darsang Kachharis speak of themselves as Bhim-ni-Fsa, that is, the children of Bhima, though according to Endle, they seem to attach little value to this highly imaginative ancestry (Endle, 1911: 6–7).

In fact, there seems to be a systematic attempt to subvert or explain away the linkages of the Mahabharata with some people in the northeast as perceived by them from an earlier period. As the Manipur story shows, the break with the Mahabharata relations seems to be complete. A historian has no doubt to be rigorous in the pursuit of his craft; his methodology should be based on facts and on his broad understanding of societal processes. However, one cannot ignore the anthropological dimension, particularly of archaeology, linguistics, and oral traditions being used slowly now to reconstruct the scientific history of the pre-literate people, as is being attempted in the north-east. Perceptions of linkages among peoples and with regional and pan-Indian traditions have been documented by anthropologists, and this is a resource that cannot be ignored. In fact, such anthropological inputs are required to reconstruct the people's view of the larger society, no matter how weak the historical foundations might be. If the Bodos have a view of their relationship with pan-Indian traditions, this cannot be described as something imaginary but has to be seen as people's efforts to link with historical traditions.

IV

The Mahabharata describes the Jambudvipa as a cluster of communities which are homogeneous and occupying specific territories (janapadas). Later these communities broke up into segments. For example, the Abhiras were stratified into the four varna categories of Abhira Brahmana, Abhira Kshatriya, Abhira Vaishya, and Abhira Sudra. The Gaddis and Pangawals of Himachal Pradesh still have Brahmana and Rajput segments who can intermarry. The People of India project shows how all regions of India, big and small, are in a microcosm multi-ethnic, multilingual, and multi-regions. And yet, there is a good deal of sharing of traits, biological and cultural, within a region. In other words, the Mahabharata notion of jana or people of a territory still endures.

To conclude, the Mahabharata is an impressive piece of ethnography. It is not comprehensive in the sense in which modern ethnography is. But it is vibrant. It covers the human surface of India in terms of description which is no doubt scanty, and relationship with communities which is interesting both on the battlefield and outside of it. Above all, it explores the ethnic diversity of the land.

There is a continuity in ethnographic traditions which links up the Mahabharata with the present-day endeavours to understand the extraordinary range of diversities—biological, linguistic, and cultural—and also the dynamic process of interaction among the people of India. The Mahabharata material, therefore, is an integral part of the evolving traditions of Indian ethnography and will always remain relevant to its understanding.

3

Manu and Contemporary
Indian Ethnography*

Manu, by far the best known codifier of laws of the ancient period, has exercised a profound influence on social history, on the course of Indian ethnography, particularly on colonial and Indian ethnographers and other social scientists, as also on social activists who have lambasted him. He has projected a profile of ethnography which needs to be reassessed in the light of new findings in ethnography, particularly those under the People of India (PoI) project, 1985–92, undertaken by the Anthropological Survey of India. In doing so, we may discuss the salient features of Manu's society, reconstruct his impact on ethnography, and evaluate his description of his society vis-à-vis the Indian society as projected by ethnography. A comparison of the two works, the *Manusamhita* and the People of India series, separated by 2,000 years, is necessary to show not only continuity and change, but also to explicate, understand, and clarify social processes.

* First published in D.N. Jha (ed.), 1995, *Society and Ideology in India: Essays in Honour of Professor R.S. Sharma*, New Delhi: Munshiram Manoharlal.

As is known, Indian society is characterized by both division and hierarchy. Manu propounds the ideology of the division of the society into varnas which he places in an order of hierarchy. Many of Manu's notions such as varna and *varnasamkara* were rooted in ancient texts and go back to an even earlier period. Historians have traced the origin of varna, and its evolution into jati from the Vedic period onwards. These notions were not unique to the brahmanical system, but were shared by the Buddhist and Jain systems as well. So was the notion of *karma varnasamkara*—deviance from the work ethic. The notion of hierarchy is similarly ubiquitous. What lends significance to Manu, more than to any other codifier of laws, is that he and his school of codifiers systematically expound their social philosophy, uphold brahmanical supremacy, seek to instill a sense of degradation through the concept of varnasamkara, and perpetuate inequality. Manu's notion of varna and varnasamkara and many of the rituals like *somskara* remain crucial to the brahmanical regulation of Hindu society.

We shall now briefly discuss the salient features of Manu's society which seem to be important from an anthropological point of view. Manu recognizes diversities. He enjoins respect for the gods and Brahmanas of the conquered country (VII. 201), and for the laws and customs of the inhabitants (VII. 203).

The ethnographic world of Manu has four distinct categories of communities. The first is the territorial category of communities living on the borders or on the fringes of Manu's Aryavarta such as Andhra, Dravida, Darada, Kirata, Saka, Yavana, and even Anga and Vaideha. Second, there are the jatis with distinct occupations such as the artisan groups of carpenters, weavers, and tailors. Third, there are the people of the four varnas. Fourth, there are communities particularly of the mixed origins who stand outside the varna system. There are in all about a hundred of them.

The ethnographic world of Manu was relatively small in terms of its geography. Many speak of Brahmavarta as lying between the two divine rivers, Saraswati and Drsadvati (II. 17), Madhyadesha lying between the Himavata and the Vindhya to the east of *prayaga* (II. 21), and Aryavarta lying between the two mountains and extending as far as the eastern and western oceans (II. 22). Two thousand years after Manu, the data generated by the PoI project put the number of communities with all other territorial segments and subgroups at 4,635. There are, in addition, nearly 65,000 segments such as *gotras*, clans and lineages, synonyms, surnames, and titles. The ethnographic universe is no longer confined to Aryavarta or Madhyadesha, but to the whole of Bharata, a concept which crystallized about three hundred years after Manu. The Andhras and Biharts (Magadhas) are known today as linguistic and territorial groups in the regions other than their own. Varna is not found to be ubiquitous as Manu would like us to believe, and there is much greater flexibility about the perception and placement of jatis. Social mobility too is far more dynamic than the rigid laws of Manu postulated.

Like all such lists of communities given in the other Sanskrit works, Manu's list is a mix of what may in the present parlance be called varna and jati categories, territorial and ethnic categories of people. Manu projects essentially the ethnographic world of north India, particularly north-west India, and generally of caste, economic roles of communities, hierarchy, and stratification. Manu focuses on the textual notion of the kinship system of the north, particularly the north-west, but ignores village exogamy of this area. He ignores the entire world of consanguinity of south, central, and western India.

Manu describes varnaas a homogeneous category. It appears that while in the case of the Brahmanas, he describes segments like the ritually high placed *srotriyas, upadhyayas* (teachers), *acharyas,* and so on, he does not seem to be aware of the existence of differentiation based on territory and status in the case of the other varnas. The Kshatriyas, Vaishyas, and Sudras are treated as monolithic which they were not. In fact, Manu deals in the same amorphous way with various other territorial categories like the Andhras, Dravidas, Magadhas, and others. This raises a question. The populations of India of which emerged the varna and later jatis have been described as more or less a homogeneous mixture. This position is however not accepted today as growing evidence suggests the existence of a variety of population groups which entered India from time to time. Some of these groups maintained their identity while others lost it. The processes of both fusion and division have been at work. Larger territorial categories such as the Abhira and Furijara broke up into occupational jatis. Much the same processes can be seen at work among the Meenas, Gaddis, Pangwals, and some other jatis even today. There was also the counter-vailing process of fusion of smaller groups into a larger whole. Caste was a cluster of endogamous jatis which were sometimes genetically different population groups; groups and subgroups, clans, gotras, and lineages merged to form larger categories in many cases.

Probably the best known dimension of Manu's schema is the theory of varnasamkara. The notion of purity of *vamsa* and the need to maintain it had emerged in the post-Vedic period. Arjuna in the Bhagavadgita, which antedates Manu's work by almost three hundred years, expresses his sense of horror at the desecration of his kula if he killed his kinsmen in the battlefield. It appears that Manu tries to resolve the problem of the placement of those communities which he cannot fit into the *chaturvarna* system. Therefore, he propounds the theory of varnasamkara to account for those who are supposed to be the progeny of the people who belong to more than one varna but have no place in it. The theory of varnasamkara could be looked at as an attempt to place at lower level these people supposedly born of hypergamous and hypogamous relationships among the members ofvarnas,and also from an ideological point of view as an attempt to understand the bicultural structure of the society in its entirety existing at the time of Manu. There was obviously an attempt to instil a sense of inferiority among these people because they had been assigned a lowly position. The varnasamkara categories certainly stood outside the chaturvarna system.

There is a biological dimension to the theory of varnasamkara as well. While Manu is emphatic about the purity of the varnas, he elabo-rates on the structure and processes of the varnasamkara. In fact, both varna and varnasamkara categories encompass a range of biological variations, as the structure of most of the Indian populations suggests even today. Manu, in spite of laying down a stringent code of con-duct and social norms, recognized resilience in mating and marriage practices. He notices the limited degree of *niyoga* for the purpose of continuing a lineage alone. He mentions both hypogamy and hyper-gamy as existential practices, even though the latter is not favoured.

Manu probably was acutely aware of biological mixing of the peoples in his days.

Many scholars have read racism into Manu's notion of varna and varnasamkara. However, such was the influence of Manu's writing on ethnography that the upper crust of the Hindu society made up of the Brahmanas, Kshatriyas, etc., was identified with the Caucasoid stock, and the lower categories of the populations were supposedly derived from the Australoid. Even in popular folklore, a Brahmana was described as fair complexioned, tall, and sharp featured. H.H. Risley (1981) discoverd another racial category called the Dravidian which was later found to be a linguistic and not a racial category. But much harm had been done already. The racial Dravidian theory provided grist to the separatist mill, and the Brahmanas in Tamil Nadu came to be regarded as belonging to a different racial stock. It was much later that the physical anthropologists found the Brahmanas of Tamil Nadu as belonging to the same gene pool as the non-Brahmana populations of the state, or at least closer to them rather than to their mythical ancestors from the north or the west.

Some anthropologists still continue with the theory of racial identification even though it has been discarded. From 1950 onwards, there has been an explosion of information on the biological heterogeneity of Indian populations, which strikes at the root of the concept of caste as a gene pool and of varna as a racial category. It is now an established fact that an ethnic identification of people of India at an all-India level is not possible. There are significant differences in the anthropometrics and genetic profiles among populations inhabiting different regions. In fact, as biological studies of Indian populations today suggest, most of the people of India are highly mixed in terms of morphological and genetic traits. The anthropologists tell us that variation in such traits, which are the result of mixing of peoples, is more within a community than between communities. There is a clustering of such traits at regional levels shared by most of the communities within a region.

The theory of varna and varnasamkara influenced the ethnographic tradition, both in the pre-colonial and the colonial phase. Those who wrote on Hindu society such as Alberuni and Abul Fazl took note of the varna system. In the colonial period the ethnographers, many of them steeped in the Oriental tradition, have taken literally Manu and his theory of varna and varnasamkara. There was an attempt to foist the theory of varnasamkara on many communities placed low in the social hierarchy. Works in local languages were written based on the *Manusamhita*. One such book quoted by Risley (1981) was *Jati Prakash* which reproduces the *Manusamhita* in the context of Bengali society. In fact, *Jati Prakash* and works of this genre continued to bear the impact of Manu's ideas on varna and varnasamkara.

However, it was during the ethnographic survey of the communities of India from 1885 onwards that attempts were made to explore Manu's ideas on varnasamkara. A scrutiny of this material presents an interesting pattern. It was in eastern India, where the survey was conducted by Risley, himself a great scholar and Orientialist, that the theory of varnasamkara was located among the largest number of communities who traced their origin to the mixing of castes such as the Conala, Namasudra, Dhoba, Dhanuk, and Kaibarta. As one moved to western, central, and southern India, the number of such people invoking their mixed origin became fewer.

In course of the generation of data for the PoI, we came across only a few examples of communities recalling their origin from the mixing of varna categories. Such self-perception would reflect partly the textural material and partly the process of Sanskritization and work among them seeking to establish their linkages with the communities placed above. The Jati Puranas are replete with instances of mixed origins within the higher jatis to explain internal hierarchy and gradation. There are stories of Brahmanas, such as sections of the Modh Brahmanas of Gujarat, who married girls from lower orders, and preserved their jati, even though they were placed at a lower level.

As one goes through the *Manusamhita*, one gets the impression that Manu is concerned more with norms which are evidently connected with ideology rather than with behaviours, and that he is far too concerned with constructing a conceptual framework than with social reality. In the process he reconstructs the social reality. There are reasons to believe that the society he lived in, like any other society with which Manu was concerned, was only less heterogeneous than our society today. The Brahmanas, described as a homogeneous lot as a varna, have as many as more than 120 jatis today. The Kshatriyas, who have all but disappeared, are invoked by a number of communities, particularly the Rajputs, who control land and the apparatus of power in many parts of the country still. There has been a great deal of social mobility among the Sudras and Vaishyas today. In fact, Manu himself recognizes the possibility of social mobility in terms of the possible transformation of a Sudra into a Brahmana. The census data of 1872–1941 reveal the extraordinary range of mobility in society, the changing perception of the varna categories about themselves and their relationship with others, the attempts by their segments to move up the social scale, and so on.

It is interesting to note that even the most savage aspect of Manu's injunctions, namely those relating to stringent punishment to be meted out to the Sudras, Chandelas, and so on, is found to exist even today. For example, the Khamti of Arunachal Pradesh has different grades of punishment to be awarded for the same offence committed by different segments of populations, hierarchically placed in their society, where the royalty/nobles forming the upper crust get away lightly while the commoners are punished heavily.

Manu seems to have ignored and even underestimated the processes of mobility in a social system, and the fact that a community is vibrant and an ever moving entity. The Chandelas have been projected by him and others as the original men living outside the main village settlements, despised and held in contempt, practising a range of occupations such as removing carcass, and making baskets: Risley (1981) cites the description given by Manu and various other authorities of the Chandelas of Bengal calling themselves Namasudra, but distinguishes between the higher division of this caste and the lower one who were called Chandela by the first and who in turn applied the name to the Dom. Risley describes the then occupation of these people as being boating and cultivation. At the time he gives this synchronic view of the Chandelas, the Namasudras, in fact, were rapidly moving forward in a spectacular manner. They were emerging as one of the two dynamic peasant communities, the other being the Rajbanshis. They even aspired to the status of the Brahmana and procured a *vyavastha* to that effect. In course of the ethnographic survey of the nineteenth century, the Chandelas were discovered only in Bengal and Orissa. A small group of people still identify themselves as Chandelas in Orissa. Our study of them also shows that, while they are placed low, they have not been a static category. They are a dynamic people engaged in a variety of occupations as peasants, agricultural labourers, pisciculturists, etc, and are involved in an effort to achieve a higher social status which has not been without success. The Namasudras are today an upwardly mobile, economically dynamic, and an important segment of the rural community in Bengal.

Manu's description of the Brahmanas is also far too idealized. The Brahmana has been described as the lord of all castes, the highest on earth, the lord of all created beings, the custodian of the sacred law (I.99). He alone can teach and cannot take up any job other than that of a preacher. And yet, Manu does not deny the possibility that the sons of a Brahmana could be engaged in a profession, which is unworthy of a Brahmana. Such a formation of brahmanical roles does not take into account the compulsions of an agrarian economy, the role of the market, or the network of larger relationships which casts the Brahmana in roles other than those of a preacher or priest. The Brahmanas founded kingdoms too. The ethnographic data, particularly those collected under the PoI project, shows that today they are widely involved in agriculture as peasants, in the public services, in the industry including the leather industry, trade and money lending. In fact, there has been a sharp decline in recent years in the role of the Brahmana as a priestly class. They are not the dominant community in many parts particularly in the west and even within the Brahmanas, such as the Nagar and Anavil, the priestly segments are placed lower than the agriculturists and traders, even though their ritual superiority is generally conceded.

Manu enjoins the first marriage of the twice-born men to be with women within equal castes but allows for subsequent marriages according to the order of the castes (III. 13). He does not uphold monogamy and allows for polygamy. This is contrary to the findings of the PoI project which shows that a vast majority of Indians are monogamous while 19.4 per cent of the communities allow sororal and non-sororal polygamy. While Manu recognizes endogamy generally and insists that the sons should marry within their own varna, he, as mentioned earlier, deals with a number of possibilities as far as mating and marriage are concerned. He is however very clear that there should be no remarriage of a Brahmana widow. He permits *niyoga* with the brother-in-law or the *spinda* of the husband in case of one son, and even allows junior levirate (IX. 120), but does not seem to recognize senior levirate or polyandry that was prevalent in many communities in northern India and elsewhere.

The entire thrust of his argument is in the direction of perpetuating the family or the lineage. For him the seed is more important than the field. The metaphor of the seed and the earth goes back to the period before Manu. It is interesting to note that this symbolism of biological reproduction and sexual relation of production which is a very old one is widespread in peasant and tribal societies in many regions of the country. It is related to patriarchal authority and the patrilineal system. The children belong to the father. The principle of the patrilineal system regulates the right of succession and the pattern of inheritance. The women have only a right to maintenance. The woman is projected as an unequal partner in the process of human reproduction, which explains her subordinate role in the management of productive resources and household matters. The PoI project has generated an enormous amount of data on the low statuses and unequal rights of women. In spite of women contributing significantly to family income through their participation in economic activities, their role in management of resources is very small. Similarly, their role in religion and ritual is correspondingly less, except in matters of rituals which are exclusively mediated by women.

Manu upholds the patrilineal system. In matters of inheritance hedoes not seem to make any distinction between a son's son and a daughter's son. However, a mother's property can equally be shared by uterine brothers, and the maternal grandfather can make a gift to the granddaughter. Except for these vestiges of a possible matrilineal inheritance, Manu seems to be totally unaware of the matrilineal system. Today this system survives not only among the Khasis and Garos and cognate tribal groups in the north-east but also among the Tulu-speaking communities in the south and in the Lakshadweep Islands; matrilineal households reportedly survive in remote parts of Kerala also. More widespread are the remnants of the possible matrilineal system spread all over central and southern India and elsewhere, whereby the daughter inherits the movable property of the mother and the unmarried woman has a right to maintenance, and othger such privileges.

Manu extols the merit of *kanyadana,* the practice of the gift of the daughter in marriage, but also allows bride price. This is known as the *asura* right where the bridegroom receives a maiden after having given as much wealth as he can afford to the kinsmen and to the bride herself according to his own will (III. 31). The bride price may also consist of a cow or a bull (III. 27–9). The PoI project reports the prevalence of bride price among the tribal and a few other communities (15 per cent), and also notes a large number of cases in which both dowry and bride price are still paid (7 per cent).

Contrary to general impression, Manu provides for all kinds of food, vegetarian and non-vegetarian, for the sustenance of the vital spirits (V. 23–8). The meat has to be sprinkled with water and made holy with the recitation of mantras. He clearly states that 'there is no sin in eating meat, in drinking spirituous liquor and carnal intercourse which is the natural way of creating human beings', but advocates total abstention, because it brings great rewards, and heavenly bliss (V. 56, 48–9). According to the findings of the PoI project, the vegetarian accounts for only a 20 per cent of the communities even though a higher value attaches to vegetarianism.

The operative word in Manu's scheme of social division is *sapinda* which ceases only with the seventh person in the ascending and descending lines (V. 60) and gotra or *sagotra* which are brahmanical concepts adopted by a number of non-brahmanical communities. There are also a number of native categories of social division regulating particularly marriage, sex, and kinship.

The various forms of relationships that Manu envisaged cut across the four varnas. The PoI project has yielded some data on hypergamous and hypogamous forms of relationship across varnas. Such forms of hypergamy and hypogamy account for nearly 2 to 4 per cent of communities in the Himalayas particularly. Modern sociologists today speak of them not so much in terms of hypergamy and hypogamy across varna categories as in terms of hypergamy and hypogamy across segments within the same jati. These segments are placed again in an order of hierarchy. They have a commensal but not an equal connubial relationship. An impressive documentation on this form of relationship exists today. With the spread of education, improvement in economic conditions, levelling up of the position of poorer segments within a caste which are becoming more equal sub-groups, endogamy is breaking up. Endogamy at the level of jati or cluster of jatis (caste) is emerging andcaste is consolidating its position as a political entity.

Manu prescribes specific occupations for some of the communities (listed in the Appendix). Of the rest, which are like generic categories, he does not seem to know enough. Many anthropologists have found in the specification of such economic roles of jatis both the origin of jatis and their integration. As N.K. Bose says:

If we read the Manusamhita carefully, we see what pains were taken to define the exact occupation of different *jatis*. Every *jati* had a particular occupation assigned to it, this being guaranteed by public opinion, and in former times, perhaps by the State. The integrity of the economic organization was thus maintained intact. It is interesting to observe that *jatis* were permitted to change their occupation in times of distress; but more strictness was enjoined in regard to the trading and labouring castes than in the case of the ruling or priestly castes. (Bose, 1941)

Bose goes on to describe how the Juangs after having taken to rope making a la Manu got integrated with the neighbouring society (through the mechanism of the market).

Historians have delineated the processes of the transformation of the varna to jati, based on textual material, in which there are more references to the former, with references to such jati categories as *hina jati* being relatively few. Manu also describes fully varna and varna-categories rather than the occupation-based jatis. However, the study of jatis in recent years in terms of ecology, and the close relationship of jatis to resources point to the possibility of jatis rather than varna being the primary unit of social formation. The different eco-regions of India have their own hierarchy of jatis, in varying degrees of control over the resources, and relationships of various jatis determine the process of control and exploitation of such resources.

From this vantage point of social research, varna seems to be an imposition of the brahmanical system as it gradually got established in different parts of India. It does not command the same degree of awareness and recognition in different parts of the country however. For instance, at the all-India level 68.5 per cent communities are aware of the varna system and only 52.6 per cent recognize it. Out of these only 7.8 per cent place themselves as Brahmanas, 15.8 per cent as Kshatriyas, 9.4 per cent as Vaishyas, and 29.1 per cent as Sudras. There is an overlap in perceptions. There is also an interesting pattern of regional variation.

There is yet another significant dimension to this. Social scientists have blown up the varna system into an all-India frame of reference within which different jatis from different parts of the country relate themselves to one another. Communication and dissemination of information have also made this interaction possible. According to some scholars, the scheduled castes or at least some of them are outside the varna system. Some of the scheduled castes call themselves Panchama, or of the fifth varna in Andhra Pradesh. The PoI data however show that a substantial number of the scheduled caste communities (70.2 per cent) now place themselves as Sudras within the varna system. Here again, regional variation has to be considered. Most of the scheduled castes in southern states and Madhya Pradesh consider themselves to be out of the varna system. But again, most of them in western and central and southern India place themselves within the system. This could be due to the anti-Brahmana movement and spread of Dalit ideology in the southern and central states.

A significant aspect of Manu's ethnography is that he provides for relaxation of commensal norms in times of famine and other social crises. The set of rules that he lays down form his concept of *apaddharma*. However, it appears that these rules were often not followed, in spite of the pandits invoking Manu, and people were excommunicated for violating commensal norms. Those who were thus excommunicated sometimes merged to form a new caste, for example, the Chhatarkheya during the Orissa famine of 1986. This raises the question of the validity of Manu's prescriptions in times of crises. It appears that each community has its own set of commensal norms which is unique to it and which is integral to its identity. Therefore, any violation of the norms would invite excommunication, no matter how compelling the circumstance was for doing so.

It is one of the paradoxes of the *Manusamhita*, as it is of similar Sanskrit classics, that after having prescribed the most stringent, even savage, forms of regulations, degrading a substantial number of people and seeking to freeze them in a state of inequality, Manu proceeds towards the end of the book to describe the state of supreme bliss. He talks of the undifferentiated Self after having described the most differentiated forms of social organization and social norms.

He who sacrifices to the self (alone), equally recognizing the self in all created beings and all created beings in the self becomes self-luminous (XII. 91). He pervades all created beings in the five forms, and constantly makes them, by means of birth, growth, and decay, revolve like wheels (XII. 124). He who thus recognizes the self through the Self in all created beings becomes equal (minded) towards all, and enters the highest state, Brahman (XII. 125).

Of course, such a state of realization is prescribed for only the twice-born man but the spirit itself is all pervasive, equal towards all. It is this aspect of the *Manusamhita* that was attacked by social reformers and activists. Mahatma Gandhi upheld the varna system but rejected jati. B.R. Ambedkar attacked both because they contained the seeds of inequality and injustice (Ambedkar, 1987–90). Copies of the *Manusamhita* are burnt these days as ugly symbols of Brahmanism are enshrined in this work. In the process, many positive features of the Sanskrit culture, mediated by the Brahmanas and by others, are overlooked. With the Supreme Court upholding reservation for the backward classes, jati has returned to the centre of the stage in modern administration and politics, where it always was in some form or the other. Therefore, a serious study is called for to understand the highly complex societal and cultural processes attempted by works such as Manu's.

4

The Indigenous Tradition
Varna Ratnakar *and its Ethnography**

Every major civilization has an ethnic universe of its own. It is generally constructed by people from outside, travellers and geographers, or by scholars and rulers from within, or by both. India has a long tradition of a bare listing of peoples in lexicons and providing occasionally a short description of communities in literary sources and the Puranas that constitute the indigenous sources of ethnography.

In this chapter we will discuss the ethnographic dimension of *Varna Ratnakar* (hereafter referred to as *VR*), a fourteenth-century classic work edited by Suniti Kumar Chatterjee and Babua Mishra (1940). The Asiatic Society of Bengal has been requested by the highest literary body of the country to bring out a re-issue in recognition of the literary and historical value of this Maithili classic.

The author of this book, Kavishekharacharya Jyotirishwara Thakur, was deeply involved in the life and activities of his period. He wrote two other books, *Dhurta Samagam* and *Panchashayak*. The latter

* Based on a paper first published in Hetukar Jha (ed.), 2002, *Perspectives on Indian Society and History: A Critique*, New Delhi: Manohar Publications.

was on the lines of Vatsyayana's *Kamasutra*, describing, among other things, the characteristics of women in different parts of the country. The influence of eroticism is also evident in *VR*. Thakur had a zest for living and possessed a holistic view of life which was shared by life-affirmative principles of the traditions of Mithila, its philosophy of *nyaya* and its *kamakanda*, its tradition of *shakti* worship and Tantra. He was a Vedic priest and linguist.

Chatterjee (Chatterjee and Mishra [eds], 1940) describes *VR* as the oldest work in prose in Maithili literature, a window on life at the court, which was in 'intimate touch with the commonalty', and a 'valuable commentary on the epigraphic and other literary records of the contemporary and earlier period'. It is an 'all-embracing compendium of life and culture in medieval India' based on information collected from textual sources in Sanskrit and from a lifetime of observation of Mithila. The author claims that he was an observer and a participant. He deftly uses the Maithili word *dekhu* or 'observe' in this connection. This work can also be seen as one of the many works of compendia (or *ratnakara*) written in the period, according to Chatterjee. Its format is suggestive. It is divided into eight chapters called *kallol*, or waves or streams which merge into the ocean or ratnakara. Set in the first quarter of the fourteenth century, it was composed in the capital of a kingdom which was relatively independent. The author describes life at the court, the market, and the processes of urbanization; he is equally familiar with rural life as evident from his description of jatis.

The authors have used the term 'varna' in the title of the book. The word has been used in more sense than one. It is meant to be a description or an order or a schema or arrangement. Varna has also been used to denote colour. In Vidyapati, slaves of different skin colours fetched different prices. It has also been used in terms not only of social classes or *jati*, but also in terms of ecological and cultural spaces, which is understandable in a compendium like this. Thus, there are descriptions of various rivers, oceans, pilgrim centres, days and nights, seasons and so on, juxtaposed with the textual material on various types of instruments, music, dress and ornaments, puranas, and so on. In later literature, varna rather than jati was used more frequently. Later, varna was used extensively for jati; still later, varna and jati was used interchangeably. In popular parlance, jati was used more often in parts of eastern India for all categories of communities including Muslims and linguistic groups.

However, a shortcoming of the text of the work available today is that it is incomplete; seventeen out of seventy-seven folios are missing including numbers one to nine which in all probability dealt with the locale of the work, the nation of Bharat or Mithila, and quite a number of communities of the *mandjati* category as also others. Therefore, one can only speculate on these missing links. At one level, this work can be seen as the epitome of the identity of Mithila and its people. In current literature, identity is an all-embracing concept defined by territory, language, dress and ornaments, cuisine, and other indicators. As the first few pages are missing, one can only guess at the author's problem description of Bharat and Mithila. Bharat as a term has been in use from a very early period, and is also to be found in medieval literature. Shankar Deo of Assam, who travelled to Puri and visited Kabir's *mazzar* at Magakar, saluted Bharat in one of his compositions. *VR*, as will be discussed later, has an all-India perspective. In its earlier incarnation, Mithila was Vaishali Vaideha, which had emerged as a large, distinct politico-cultural region very early in history. During the early Gupta perod, Videha and Vaishali merged to form the new and larger administrative and political unit of Tirabhukti (AD 329) or Tirhut, as the whole of north Bihar came to be known as later. Tirhut is also mentioned in medieval Persian sources. References to Mithila in vernacular literature generally describes it as a cultural region lying south of the Himalayas encompassing the terai of Nepal and the plains of north Bihar, bounded by the rivers Gandak in the west and Kosi in the east which constituted the boundary with Bengal. The present Mithila converges on the four linguistic–cultural regions of Angika, Vajjika, Bhojpuri, and Magahi.

The fourteenth century witnessed the flowering of the Maithili language, *VR* being one of the earliest works in it. The following century, the age of Vidyapati, was described as the golden period of Maithili which influenced the literary traditions of Bengal. Mithila lay across the routes of Bengal and therefore a part of it, Darbhanga, was known as the doorway to north Bengal (*dwarabanga*). The etymology of Darbhanga, the earliest reference to which is traced to the twelfth century AD, is also said to have been derived from the two words, *daru* and *bhanga,* that is, the felling of trees as the jungle was cleared, and the area was settled or the capital established. It is interesting to note that there is a trace of forty villages peopled by the Mundas called Dalbhanga (that is, breaking in two) in Ranchi/Singhbhum districts. The Mundas circulated the twigs (*daal*) of the sal tree held sacred by them in times of revolt as a token of invitation to people to join in the battle against aliens. One does not know if there is any connection between this Austric word and Darbhanga, but if *VR* is any evidence, Mithila was lush green, with a rich variety of fauna and flora which, had they survived, would have been an environmentalist's delight. Migration of communities from upper India to Assam occurred along these routes. The armies, too, moved along them from Delhi or Jaunpur to Lukhanauti, and yet it is surprising that Mithila could safeguard its independence for a very long time until it was annexed by the Delhi Sultanate in AD 1324. Similarly, *VR* mentions the identity indicators of Mithila in terms of dress (*pag*) or food (rice-curd and sweets), which was consumed by all sections of people. At another level, *VR* is a combination of not only a regional listing of communities and categories, but also of a national or countrywide listing of the same. This feature was brought home to me as I compared the listing of communities given in this work with similar listings available elsewhere.

The *Arthashastra*, the *Manusamhita*, and the Mahabharata provide pan-Indian lists of communities. To these works may be added Abul Fazl's *Ain-i-Akbari* which provides a complete list of dominant lineages belonging to all castes and creeds in Akbar's empire. *VR* contains a list of communities not only of Mithila, but also of large parts of the country. In fact, it lists 201 communities. *VR* also reproduces the Sanskrit terms for regions and territories (*sthana* and *desh*) such as the Chola, Chauhan, Gaum (Gaur), Malava, Gujarat, Maharashtra, Vahal (Multan), and Sinhal; a few are unintelligible; Daahal, Marar, Khorasan, Netal, and Bot (Tibet) were added later. *VR* does not mention the cultural change in and political transformation of these regions in the medieval period. Gandhar was no longer a part of India. It also reproduces the textual list of rivers—Ganga, Yamuna, Narmada,

Saraswati, Tamraparni, Gomati, Kaushki, Agvati, Kaveri, and nu-
merous other rivers. It identifies pilgrim centres all over India up to
Setubandh and Gangasagar. These lists of rivers and pilgrim centres
constitute the fourteenth-century perspective on the Hindu universe
extending beyond the geographical limits of Mithila. The *Ain-i-Akbari*
also provides a similar picture of the world of Hindu religion extending beyond the limits of Akbar's empire, as revealed by the description
of pilgrim centres of the south.

However, *VR* is also Mithila-specific, and in this sense its listing of
communities can be compared with the regional listing of communities
available in different parts of India either in textual material or in
inscriptions including temple inscriptions. These two perspectives,
Mithila-specific and the pan-Indian one, should be kept in mind while
analysing the lists of jatis contained in the *VR*. The author mentions
two distinct categories, *mand* and *bhadra*, but the various jatis listed
by him can be classified into as many as eight categories. The first is the
category of mand jati under which he includes forty jatis. As already
discussed, this list is obviously incomplete because a few of the earlier
folios are missing. The notion of mand jatis can be compared with that
of hin jatis mentioned in early Sanskrit literature. An analysis of the
jatis suggests that they are a heterogeneous category consisting of jatis
of various statuses. Many jatis including 'service castes' in the *VR* have
been identified with present-day jatis or their segments: Tongar with
Gonpal, Dhaol with Dhaul, Dhangal with Dhangar, Bhal with Bihar,
Dhalikar with Dharkar (basket maker), and so on. It is interesting to
note that the extent of equivalence of mand jatis with present-day
jatis or their segments has been highest, compared with that of other
categories mentioned in the *VR*.

The next category is that of bhadra jatis which brings to mind the
notion of *bhadralok* prevalent in adjacent Bengal. Many jatis under
this category are evidently missing. For example, the Brahmanas with
their five sub-castes and a large number of *mool* (sect); the Karna
Kayastha groups are also missing. The Cheros, who had emerged as a
dominant ruling lineage in western Bihar and a part of northern Bihar
that lay within Mithila, are missing too. Included in this category is
the Rajputra, though *VR* mentions it separately, which again is a term

that appears in contemporary Sanskrit literature. However, Vidyapati uses the local term Rajput. *VR* lists as many as seventy-one Rajput clans, though the Sanskrit texts of the period mention only thirty-six. This could be due to the proliferation of the local jatis of Rajputs, who emerged as ruling lineages in Mithila and the adjoining regions. Of particular interest in this connection is the local Rajput jati of Lohtamia of western Bihar or of Gamharia mentioned in the *VR* which became an important ruling family in Mithila.

The third category is that of the forest tribes which includes seventeen jatis. The list is an interesting combination of textual material and local identities. For example, while the communities living in the jungles such as the Kochs, Kirats, Gond nats, Pahalias or Bahelias, Donawars and Bhatars can be identified even today in and around Mithila, others like the Bhils, Pulinds, Savaras, and Milechhas have been drawn from Sanskrit texts. These are not to be found anywhere in and around Mithila. Of these communities, of particular interest is the Kirata. In Sanskrit literature, 'kirata' has been used both in the sense of a generic category, as a community living everywhere in the hills and forests, and also as a specific category of people, probably the Indo-Mongoloids living in the Himalayas. It is in the latter sense that Bharavi in his celebrated work, *Kiratarjuniya Mahakavyam,* refers to the Kirata as the dominant community of the Himalayas whose rulers commanded respect. Suniti Kumar Chatterjee's *Kirat Janakirti* (1951) focuses on the notion of Kirata with respect to the communities of the north-east, who found the states and built up an impressive cultural system, drawing upon the then existing network of communication with the rest of the country. Recently, the Kirata has been described as a construct for Aryan discourse, the perceptions of the Kirata changing across the centuries. It has been increasingly used in Nepal and the adjoining areas to denote the autochthones, that is, the more primitive groups as distinguished from the later migrants, including the Tagadharis, other Mongoloid groups, and the untouchables in Nepal. An essentially Sanskrit concept, the term is now used to denote a non-Sanskrit or even an anti-Sanskrit identity. It should be noted that the term *mlechha* did not always denote an alien or a foreigner, or was always rigid and contemptuous in its application. It was applicable to both foreign and indigenous tribal communities, and was flexible and accommodating, resulting in the absorption of alien communities into the Indian society.

There is a category of communities which is supposed to serve the ruler. This includes the trading classes, business groups, cultivators, and the service castes—almost all 'clean' classes. Finally, the author refers to a number of communities engaged in begging or in criminal activities, known as the lumpen elements today, which were perceived as a menace to the city dwellers in those days. The description of women and the eroticism in the VR will not go down well with present-day feminists who see in them evidence of gender discrimination. Further, there is description of various classes of women such as the *nayika*, *khangi*, *veshya* (prostitutes), *nagri* (artful women), and *kulini* (old, haggard pimps) that will be considered derogatory. Women were considered lower in status, and kulinism further degraded the status of women.

It is said that the VR projects essentially the view of a society composed of what is now described as Hindu communities. There is no reference to the Yavanas of Muslims, or Islam. In fact, Tirhut or Mithila had already felt the impact of Persian culture, some elements of which were absorbed by Mithila society. For example, there are as many as twenty Arabic and Persian words in the VR. My attention has been drawn to the jati called Tuluk included in the list of mand jatis. According to some scholars, Tuluk is none other than Turk. This raises various problems including one about the absorption and ranking of Turks within the category of mand jatis. At present, Muslim communities do figure in the local hierarchy of jatis or communities in different parts of the country. In fact, the Muslim is recognized as a 'caste' in a limited sense. But was the same possible in the fourteenth century when Turkish influence was barely a hundred to a hundred and fifty years old? There is evidence that the Muslims had settled down in north Bihar, and were employed by the local Hindu chiefs in much the same way as Hindus were employed by Muslim rulers. Therefore, was it possible for the Turk to be mentioned as a mand jati in the local hierarchy? This question needs to be probed further.

The *VR* ignores the far-reaching changes in lifestyle occurring not only in Mithila but elsewhere too. The countervailing picture is provided in the *Sharaf-namah-i-Mameri*, a lexicographical work by Ibrahim Qawwam Faruqi, who had migrated from Bihar to Bengal. This work describes items of food and drink, clothes and costumes, utensils, games, etc., introduced by the Muslims. Alongside are mentioned the new classes of professionals which emerged: *bazargan* (merchant), *baazigar* (juggler), *zargar* (gold-smith), *najjar* (carpenter), *karra* (barber), and so on. This issue is linked up with the confrontation of cultures during the period under review. When Islam spread to this part of the country, as the Turko-Afghan rule was established, the existing society reacted in three ways. First, in the initial phase, as Vidyapati mentions in the *Kirtilata*, the Brahmanas were harassed. There is evidence that a Chero chief killed the son of a Sufi saint. Second, a segment of Hindu society withdrew into itself and reinforced the norms of orthodoxy as part of a self-defensive strategy. Some of the works of Mithila of this period including the *VR* could be cited as evidence of this, alongside the works of Goswami Tulsidas who simply ignores the presence of the others. Third, as the situation stabilized, there developed a better understanding of each other. Evidence of this is provided by the fact that the Hindu rulers reconstructed mosques, or gave endowments to Muslim shrines, or employed Muslims who had brought in a new technology. A synergetic process was set in motion whereby elements of Hinduism and Islamic Sufism were sought to be fused. Kabir, living in the neighbourhood of Mithila, speaks at one level of the Hindu and the Turk as separate ethnic categories with different religious symbols, the mandir and the masjid, and at another level extols the underlying unity of both in terms of spirituality or *ruhaniyat*, the oneness of God, and of values extending beyond the barriers of caste and creed.

A comparison of the list of jatis given in the *VR* and the list of jatis generated by colonial and post-colonial ethnography suggests that while a number of communities can be identified, there are quite a few others which cannot be. The communities mentioned in the *VR* have survived today either as a whole or as a sub-caste, or a segment of other communities. Many communities have moved up the social and economic ladder. For example, Donwar, which is mentioned as a forest dwelling community, is now a segment of the Bhumihar Brahmana, and the Rajput jatis have acquired a new respectability. The Dhanuk, described as hillmen, fowlers, and hunters, were later absorbed into the feudal system as housekeepers or domestic helps.

A related question that arises in connection with the interpretation of this work is whether the *VR* constitutes a model of the brahmanical view of hierarchy where some segments are looked down upon and even held in contempt. However, a broader view of the culture and society of Mithila during the medieval period is needed before passing any judgement. It would be a gross oversimplification to say that Mithila was only a centre of brahmanical orthodoxy. In fact, Mithila was marked by the convergence of various streams of thought and culture. Even within the brahmanical system there existed among authors of *smirit*s a fairly wide spectrum of views, including even a pragmatic and somewhat liberal understanding of social issues. One of them recognized the right of the Sudras to make gifts, or sell meat. Others recognized the acceptance by Brahmanas of uncooked food and even cooked food from the Sudras in times of distress. As mentioned earlier, the category of mand jatis was a heterogeneous one consisting of what may be described today as both 'clean' and 'non-clean' castes.

Mithila was a centre not only of orthodoxy but also of hetero-doxy in the past, and of Tantra and shakti worship during the period under study. This explains the prevalence of non-vegetarianism among the Brahmanas and in the brahmanical system of this region. Some of the heterodoxic aspects of traditions survive in Mithila's folklores and folk rituals. The logic ballads and Dosadh's *Salhes* deserve to be studied as alternative paradigms. *VR* mentions only the *shastric* forms of marriage and omits the *asurik* forms. Vidyapati, however, describes the *lokik* form of marriage rituals, particularly those of the *kohavar*. The kohavar rituals deserve to be studied in depth because they are mediated by women who define their space and autonomy, and subtly assert their identity and even dominance. They also symbol-ize induction into marital sexuality. There are many other 'irreverent' aspects of folk rituals including the rain-making rituals, as also of folk-lores which are a vibrant part of the people's consciousness.

Therefore, the picture of Mithila or of the country that emerges from an ethnographic study of the *VR* is one of diversities of all types—ecological, social, and cultural, standing at the centre of currents and cross-currents of political and even of market forces. It shows Mithila and even the whole country as a land inhabited by many communities. In fact, all regions of India have been a macrocosm of many influences, perceptions, and identities. This has been the essence of the Indian experience, and of the process of change and development in the country. Again, compared to Mithila of the fourteenth century, present-day Mithila, culturally rich but economically backward and impoverished, is the centre of radical social transformation, with the mand jatis in the forefront contributing what is Mithila's best known gift to the world of art—Mithila paintings.

5

Colonial Ethnography
Caste, Tribe, and Race

Information about people and knowledge of the social structure in the colonial period was derived from three interrelated streams: ethnographic surveys conducted from 1805 onwards, the gazetteers, and the censuses from 1871 to 1941. All the three streams interacted and shared a great deal in terms of administrative infrastructure, the personnel who participated in and presided over them, and the overriding need for generating information that could make governance easy and make for identification of human resources and skills for exploitation.

Ethnography of the gazetteers was an independent stream of ethnographic survey—selective, brief, abounding in stereotypes, not always flattering, collected from knowledgeable local people. District gazettes for which material was extensively used in writing the ethnographic survey reports from Madras and Bombay presidencies, and the Imperial Gazetteers of India.

Much of the knowledge of people which was generated in the colonial period was influenced by worldwide trends in ethnography and also determined by colonial needs. There is also no doubt that the colonial masters tried to highlight divisions; fissiparous colonialism introduced the notions of race, tribe, and caste, and they devised various modes of classifying populations with a view to solving social and administrative problems. This was in spite of the fact that some ethnographers noted the underlying unity of India behind its ethnographic diversities and hyped about the rise of a nation. But it will be wrong to assume that colonial ethnography invented castes in the spirit of the colonial nomenclatures of caste and tribe. Varied communities always existed in India and have been listed from the very ancient times, as mentioned above. Manu and Kautilya mention a large number of communities, most of which cannot be identified today. Regional listing of castes also existed. If the Dharma Shastras are any indication, hierarchy and division had crystallized already in the pre-colonial period. The rajas of Chhotanagpur and Orissa could upgrade individuals and families to a higher status, and these segments in course of time became endogamous groups. The *Ain-i-Akbari* identifies dominant communities in different parts of Akbar's empire that constituted its large social base. These names are strikingly familiar today.

As mentioned elsewhere, colonial census and ethnography originated in the need for information about people to facilitate their governance and to expedite the exploitation of their skills and resources. Both were thus linked by common objectives, and manned by the same administrative cadre who planned and operated the census and ethnographic surveys, and analysed and wrote out the materials generated by these gigantic bureaucratic operations on caste and tribe, their classification/categorization, occupation, ranking, and so on.

At the highest level colonial administrators like E.A. Gait, H.H. Risley, and J.H. Hutton spanned the census and ethnographic surveys and the studies undertaken by them later. In the provinces colonial officers like Russell and Hiralal continued the same traditions of participating in the census and conducting ethnographic surveys. Multiple examples of this kind may be found particularly at the district level where the officers participated in the census and wrote ethnographic notes on castes and tribes in their area, and then went on to write settlementary reports and also helped in writing gazetteers, both of which contained a good deal of ethnographic materials.

The 1881 census was the mother of colonial ethnography. The pioneer who extracted the maximum ethnographic information on the dynamic relationship among space, community, and occupation was Denzil Ibbetson, the Superintendent of Census. It was in deference to his work and status that a meeting was held in Lahore in March 1884 to consider the twenty-seven-point format of the ethnographic survey.

Ibbetson (1883) looked at the census of 1881 not only as a means of collecting information on selected subjects but as a 'sketch of salient features of native societies in the Punjab'. He had a larger view of the census. As he said in his introduction:

A census report is not light reading and men take it up not to read it through, but to obtain from it information on some definite point. It is therefore more important that it should be complete than that it should be brief and so long as its arrangement directs the students at once to the place where he will find what he wants without compelling him to wade through irrelevant matter. The fuller the information which he there finds on the subjects, the more valuable will the report [be] to him. I have therefore omitted nothing relevant that seems to me to be interesting or useful simply because it occupied space.

(Ibbetson, 1883)

Thus was census ethnography born that furnished for the first time information on a community, its internal structure, and its variations. Punjab had an ethnography that was distinct from that of other parts of the country. The census report was published in 1883. A separate volume, *Punjab Ethnography*, containing information about religions, languages, races, castes, and tribes was issued in 1883. In 1916 another volume containing ethnological information was published under the title *Punjab Castes*.

H.A. Rose built upon the foundation laid down by Ibbetson. He also avoided using physiometry but provided a little more of the ethnographic materials along the lines laid down by Ibbetson, as the Ethnographic Survey of India 1901–08 was extended to the Punjab. The material generated by the survey was presented in the format of the Ethnographic Survey. However, the Punjab material was not entirely based on an ethnographic survey like in the other provinces.

In fact, H.A. Rose's book entitled *Glossary of the Tribes and Castes of Punjab and North-west Frontier Province* (1919) continued to be based primarily on the census report of 1883 by late Denzil Ibbetson, and the census report of the Punjab of 1892 by Edward Maclagan. The Punjab chapter of colonial ethnography appears to be a little different from similar volumes on other provinces.

The methodology adopted by Ibbetson and others in other provinces was very alike. They relied on the evidence furnished by 'gentlemen' informants, and put their testimonies through repeated checks. Yet, the conceptual framework of Ibbetson ethnography was not only pioneering but also refreshing in contrast to some later ethnographers. First, as mentioned earlier, although compiled under the rubric of race, tribe, and caste, it was singularly free from the discussion of race. The exploration of race was considered by ethnographers like Risley and Crooke as one of the modes of understanding the Indian social organization. Second, Ibbetson looked at the communities in situ as they were in terms of their occupation, status, access to resources, and relationship to power. He not only studied the internal structure of the communities but also its variations. He did not go by the text only but also by the reality of the relationships. Ibbetson is also credited with a dynamic view of communities in the Punjab which was historically placed in a situation of fluidity and rapid change. For him caste was neither perpetual nor immutable. In his studies he emphasized their linkages with space, occupational mobility, heterogeneity, the dignity of the people, their zeal for life, and other characteristics.

Ethnographers earlier described all communities as tribes. The distinction between tribe and caste did not fully emerge until the census of 1901. However, though Ibbetson was aware of the all pervasiveness of caste structures and caste values, he tried to make a distinction between caste and tribe. Occupation was the primary basis of caste, reinforced by status and caste rules. A tribe was bound by the notions of 'common origin, common habitat, common customs and modes of thought' (Ibbetson, 1883: 10). A tribe, particularly a clan, was strongly linked with territory as well. Ibbetson applied the structure or category of caste to identify the social organization among the Brahmanas and the Hindu non-agricultural, mercantile castes of the Khatris, Aroras, and Baniyas who were held together by rules of endogamy, notion of purity and pollution, and so on. The concept of tribe was also applied to the agricultural castes based on the notion of common descent, to Muslim communities such as Baloch and Pathan, and to pastoral and other groups on the periphery. However, Ibbetson also describes tribal divisions within the priestly and mercantile castes, among artisans and 'menial' castes, and among women. It is obvious that the situation was fluid. Today, there are few who share his view, though they agree with Ibbetson's point on the dynamism of caste and the social situation, and the change noted by him in the meanings of such groups as Jats and Rajputs, not only historically but also ethnically. The ethnographic profile of India that emerges under the People of India project, which is close to the ethnography of Ibbetson, has community rather than tribe and caste as its focus which share a lot of traits, to a larger or lesser extent, and the tribe is a community relatively isolated, distant, and backward.

The other concerns of colonial ethnography could be briefly discussed. The colonial ethnographers and administrators romanticized the Jats. In Rose's *Glossary* we find these well-known lines by Ibbetson: '[T]he most important of the Punjab peoples ... the peculiar and most prominent product of the plains of the five rivers ... the husbandman, the peasant, and the revenue payer par excellence of the Province' (Rose, 1919). Similarly, Tod (1829) idealized the Rajputs to the neglect of the other communities, and ignored conflicting perceptions. The Jats, particularly the Sikh Jats, have proved themselves worthy of these observations, but the ethnographic scenario is much too complex, and there is an inexorable movement over time towards equality and pluralism. So there are few takers for stereotypes of communities in colonial and non-colonial literature.

Another finding of colonial ethnography was about the model of Rajputization which was ubiquitous among most of the communities of the Punjab, particularly the lowly placed ones who considered themselves descendants of Rajputs, but who had lost their status through the process of degradation that occurred in phases. The Punjab had a large Rajput population particularly in the hills. The Dalits now do not invoke this model and instead stress their identity in situ which reflects self-respect and self-confidence. The colonial ethnographers also devoted considerable space to exploring the linkages of the Khatris with the Kshatriyas and the transformation of the warriors into traders and businessmen, which has been reported from Gujarat and Rajasthan. The etymological derivative of 'Khatri' from 'Kshatriya' is indisputable as is the pre-eminent position of the Khatri in Punjabi society. But today, such transformation appears to be problematic. There is a difference between the ethos of warriors and traders. The Khatris also owned land which suggests a peasant origin. There was a section with martial surnames. The Khatris also occupied important positions as generals, administrators, and political and social leaders. Thus the Khatri seems to have a complex origin. Similarly, the linkages between Rajputs and Jats, Ahirs and Gujjars have been stressed on by ethnographers. This notion contains the seeds of an organization—the Ajgar, consisting of the Ahir, Jat, Gujjar, and Rajput—which was sought to be built up by political leaders. The difference between the Jats and Rajputs and the others were cultural rather than biological, and unity efforts broke down on the issues of sororate, *karewa* and remarriage.

The colonial administrators had a soft corner for the agricultural castes which formed the bedrock of rural society and economy, and were sensitive to their exploitation by Hindu money lenders. Therefore Punjab pioneered the Punjab Alienation of Land Act of 1900 which debarred the traditional non-agricultural castes from buying land belonging to the agricultural tribes.

All ethnographic accounts are unanimous in reporting that conversion to Islam did not make any difference to the caste status of the believers or their social customs including rules of marriage and inheritance. The only difference was the little beard that appeared on the face of the new converts as against a shaved chin, the change in name, and the rudimentary knowledge and practice of the new religion. Similarly, conversion to Sikhism entailed a lesser break with the past. But all this changed as the colonial period came to a close. The identities of the Hindu/Muslim/Sikh was well consolidated under the influence of the colonial policy of promoting orthodoxification, and under the influence of various religious movements among the three communities which led to each distancing itself from the other. Fundamentalism emerged, articulated by religious organizations, from the latter half of the nineteenth century—Anjuman among the Muslims, Arya Samaj among the Hindus, and Singh Sabha among the Sikhs. Each first reacted against the Christian missionaries and employed the missionaries' mode of polemics and their vocabulary in denouncing them, and then turned upon one another on the home ground. They also promoted social reforms. The Arya Samaj movement (1871) among the Hindus promoted education both among men and women, advocated widow remarriage, 'restored' ritual rites to women who were permitted to participate in *yagna*s, and tried to uplift some of the lowest of the low groups such as the Dom by giving them a new name, Mahasaya, and bringing them the benefits of education. The life cycle ceremonies were organized around the yagna, and were simple and inexpensive. The Singh Sabha movement (1872) that followed tried to establish the Sikh as a separate community; they denounced the Brahmanas for their betrayal of the Sikh Gurus, abjured brahminical practices, promoted education, and developed Punjabi literature. There were sharp differences among the three main communities in matters of language and script. The Muslims adopted Urdu in Perso-Arabic script, the Sikhs favoured Punjabi in Gurumukhi script, and the Hindus went for Hindi in Devanagri script. Almost a hundred years of scramble for a share in the power structure, the search for roots in the course of identity formation, and fear and mistrust distanced the three major religious communities from one another on the eve of Independence. The riots and migrations following Partition did the rest in alienating the communities. It is said that the Punjabi middle class that emerged in the colonial period was communal rather than secular, and the few educated persons in the Punjab identified themselves as Punjabis and with Punjabiyat, and both the regional identity and Indian nationalism were casualties for the time being. However, such evidence as we have now from literature and historical writings suggests that these larger identities survived and even became stronger at many levels—individual, familial, political, cultural, and so on.

Sir H.H. Risley has been regarded as the architect of colonial ethnography and its chief theorist, though there was diversity within this ethnographic tradition and other ethnographers like Denzil Ibbetson tried to blaze their own trail. Risley started with the race theory of caste, divided castes into neat racial types, the Aryan, the Dravidian, and the Mongoloid, with the higher castes belonging to the Aryan, and the intermediate caste ranks of mixed origin and lower groups mostly consisting of tribal and lower castes. Risley's theory of nasal index stands at the centre of his anthropometry: a man's social status varies in inverse ratio to the width of his nose; the finest nose shall be at the top of the hierarchy and the coarsest at the bottom (Risley, 1915). This theory is not accepted now. As D.D. Kosambi writes in his essay 'Race and Immunity in India', physical anthropometry gives less reliable results because nasal index, height and other aspects change (Kosambi, 2009). Nor is Risley's related view about Aryans and Dravidians being two distinct races acceptable. However, his work is still important for the ethnographic information on castes and tribes that he collected. Risley focused on hypergamy, female infanticide, child marriage, and so on, and linked Indian ethnography with Western ethnography, its methodology, and the main trends. Risley (1915) pitted nationalism against religion and caste, and wondered how a nation could be built without undermining religion and caste. A nation did emerge out of heterogeneity and freedom struggle but did not undermine caste and religion for the time being, but Risley did not live to see this.

Of all the ethnographers, one of the best known was W. Crooke of the Bengal Civil Service who compiled 'The Tribes and Castes of the North West Provinces and Oudh' (1896) in four volumes, before the Ethnographic Survey 1901–8 was launched in the rest of the provinces except Bengal. He came nearest to H.H. Risley in terms of methodology and content of ethnography, and worked comprehensively on the colonial ethnography of the region towards the end of the nineteenth century. Like Risley, who believed in race and in anthropometry as a tool for the understanding of social organization, Crooke was of the view that as caste had been in a state of flux, 'far from being eternal and changeless constantly subject to modification', 'the only trustworthy basis for the ethnological survey of Upper India must be based on anthropometry' (Crooke, 1974).

He was the district magistrate of Mirzapore, as part of a long stint of service, and his ethnographic work was in addition to his 'multitudinous official tasks'. He described Mirzapore as situated on the tip of the Vindhya ranges, as the last refuge of the Dravidian races (like Risley he mistook the Dravidians for a race) living in the mountainous and forest tracts stretched along the great Ganga–Yamuna valley. As he observed, these people were

... becoming rapidly Brahamanised, and will probably in a few years have lost much of what is peculiar to them and interesting to the ethnologist and student of the development of popular religion. Even now our Kols, Kharwars, Cheros and Manjhis are much less primitive people than their brethren whose manners and institutions have been analysed by Colonel Dalton, Mr. Risley and Mr. Hislop. The improvement of communication, the facility for visits to the sacred shrines of Hinduism, the Brahmanical propaganda preached by those most active of all missionaries, the Panda and the Purohit, the Jogi and the sanyasi[,] will before long obliterate much of the primitive ideas which they will still retain though in a modified form. (Crooke, 1974)

Crooke's fear has not been proved right, and today all communities are conscious of their identity. Like Risley and others, Crooke depended for information on the 'much cordial co-operation of district officers and a large body of native gentlemen in the plains'. For investigation he drew upon such sporadic ethnographic information as existed from the North Western Provinces and Oudh and other areas. Crooke was probably the only ethnographer to discuss methodological problems such as 'the reticence of the lower caste', or 'the movement among many castes towards claiming a higher status than is usually accorded to them and manipulation of textuality and the variation of the local patios from district to district.' He therefore 'avoided as far as possible discussions of topics which are likely only to cause pain to sections of the people whose pertinence to a higher rank or origin are, to say the least[,] disputed' (Crooke, 1974).

Crooke was soon to discover that anthropometry was no guide to social organization. As he later observed, there was only a very slight material difference between the 'highest and the noblest born

Aryan' and the lowest and 'the humblest born Dravid'. He, therefore, concluded that 'the racial origin of all must have been similar and the foundation on which whole caste system in India is based is that of function and not upon real or appreciable difference of blood' (Crooke, 1974).

In the colonial period, the listing of castes started in the Madras presidency in 1806 and passed through various phases till the ethnographic survey of the large territory produced the most voluminous ethnographic output. The seven volumes on *Castes and Tribes of Southern India* (first published in 1909) authored by Edgar Thurston, who was assisted by K. Rangachari, are unique for many reasons. First, these volumes were prepared under the aegis of the Ethnographic Survey of India launched in 1901. Second, the survey was carried out not by British administrators, as in other parts of India, but by the musicologists located in the Madras Museum, who had been carrying on such studies sporadically since 1894, particularly among the tribes of the Nilgiri Hills at high altitudes 'when thermometer stood high in Madras city'. Third, the survey drew heavily on the published literature, including district manuals and district gazettes. Information was also sought from 'representative men' and through 'own inquires' and 'replies to the stereotyped series of questions'. It was noted that the replies were not 'entirely satisfactory, as they broke down both in accuracy and detail'. However, direct inquires by the officers connected with the survey were restricted to 'three months on circuit in camp, during which the dual functions of the survey—the collection of ethnographic and anthropometric data—were carried out in the peaceful isolation of the Jungals in villages, and in mofussil (up-country) towers'. These wandering expeditions afforded 'ample evidence that delay in carrying through the scheme for the survey would have been fatal' (Thurston, 1987). Thurston also left a hilarious account of the encounter with the people who were surveyed and measured.

Thurston's ethnographic survey contains a detailed report on the many, if not all, communities of south India, alphabetically arranged. South India subsumed what was then commonly known as the Madras presidency and its dependencies, which included small feudatory states and also the large native states of Travancore and Cochin but not Mysore (except for anthropometric measurements).

The ethnography of Karnataka as it is constituted today consists of the materials compiled by Thurston, Enthoven, and Sirajul Hassan for the people living in the Madras presidency, the Bombay presidency, and the Nizam's dominion covering Hyderabad respectively. However, its core is formed by the ethnographic survey of the Mysore state undertaken by the late L.K. Ananthakrishna Iyer, who alongside Sarat Chandra Roy shared the distinction of being the father of Indian ethnography. He was an ethnographer par excellence in the survey tradition. Iyer was more than an ethnographer actually. He was deeply aware of the macro historical processes of change. Therefore, he devoted one full volume on Mysore to describing the context in which the communities lived. He was also a master of a simple and lucid style that makes his books still a pleasure to read. His works have remained a solid benchmark for all subsequent studies of the communities he had surveyed. There are no two opinions about authenticity of the highest order of the material he produced. As R.R. Marett says in his introduction to the Mysore volume:

The present work then, may, in my opinion, be regarded as a model of such sociological research as an Indian student can undertake for the lasting benefit and renown of India, limiting itself severely to the level of description; it puts on record the characteristic habits of the very various units composing the population of an entire State, and affords a remarkably clear view of its social stratigraphy from top to bottom ... The author has been most careful to collect all available information concerning the origins of each ingredient in the mixture, giving likewise for what they may be worth, the legends wherein such antecedents are set forth with the aid of the popular imagination eked out, it may be with some genuine folk memory ... It is further to be noted that thoroughness of treatment is attained not only by detailing the customs of each social group in turn, but likewise by submitting each set of customs to analysis under a series of identical categories. The prime object, no doubt, is to secure that nothing shall be overlooked in a particular context, even if in similar contexts much the same has to be said over again ... The book is full of admirable photographs of typical groups, but in a figurative sense of the term its whole purpose might be said to be photographic. With the cold precision of a mechanical eye, it registers everything brought within its shifting focus, so that science can have no doubt about the evidential value of its data.

(Marett in Iyer, 1935)

The methodology that Iyer followed for his Mysore survey was a little different however. The basic work here had already been done by H.V. Nanjundayya as the Superintendent of Ethnography in the usual administrative way. He must have sent administrative circulars around to the *tehsildars* to collect information. These tehsildars and other local functionaries were steeped in rural life and could be depended on to send a reasonably authentic account of the communities they were called to report about, but Iyer carefully revised and edited the thirty-four monographs published between 1903 and 1918 in the light of fresh additional material added by him. He found the notes on fifty tribes and castes mostly fragmentary. As he says: 'But most of them were mere fieldnotes in pencil on a few topics out of which nothing could be done. If these tribes and castes were to be dealt with, it was clear that a fresh investigation into manners and customs of all these tribes was imperative' (Iyer, 1935).

That Iyer had meticulously surveyed the ethnographic terrain is borne out by the fact that under the People of India project we found a good majority of the communities living in the erstwhile Mysore states substantially covered by him. Iyer generally adhered to the twenty-seven-point format drawn up in 1885 by H.H. Risley and two others for the ethnographic survey of India, but simplified this format into a fourteen-point one, which covered the origin and tradition of a community, the internal structure, marriage customs, inheritance, religion, occupation, life-cycle ceremonies, dress, ornaments, and so on. Iyer, also like the others, borrowed Nesfeld's occupational categories of the people of India, but generally stuck to the ethnographic format. There was no clear distinction between tribe and caste until the census of 1901. True to the ethnographic tradition, he gave a greater weightage to the description of life-cycle ceremonies. And like other ethnographers of his time, he treated the caste or tribe as an isolate and did not describe its interaction and linkages with other groups. Internal structure of a caste was described in some detail. The differences among various sub-groups in terms of myths of origin, ritual performances, and so on, were however not touched upon. No account was given of change and development.

The ethnographic survey of the Bombay presidency in the colonial period was carried out under the aegis of the Ethnographic Survey of India, 1901–09. Owing to the cessation of the meagre funding, the survey became dependent on the voluntary labour of the part-time superintendent, and of scholars like D.R. Bhandarkar and B.A. Gupte who worked as honorary assistants. There were 'gentlemen' working as 'honorary correspondents' as well. Another source of information was the local communities organized by the superintendent during the census who supplied materials of 'volume and importance'. The draft reports were circulated for comments. However, the survey drew upon the materials available in the pages of the *Gazetteer of the Bombay Presidency* compiled by the late Sir James Campbell, which later invited the charge of plagiarism against Enthoven (discussion with A.M. Shah). However, Enthoven explains his position candidly. The termination of financial support left him with no option but to depend on voluntary support and draw on the original district accounts which he described as 'remarkable both for their fulness and accuracy' and as the main source of information. He acknowledges that much of the work of the survey consisted of the 'rearrangement of these materials' (Enthoven, 1975).

The limits of the survey were acknowledged. Depending on the size of the populations (100,000–100,000 to 5,000–below 5,000) the 500 tribes and castes were dealt with fully, partly, and 'superficially' by merely arranging the materials on the lines of the ethnographic questions. Not all of the communities were thus covered equally and uniformly, the extent of their coverage varying according to their number. The ethnographic survey covered (i) those who were described as a unit based on common descent, (ii) castes described as a social unit founded on common occupation, common residence, common language, and common political control, and (iii) sects described as units based on religion (Enthoven, 1975).

The ethnographic survey made a distinction between tribe and caste, identifying the first with 'a unit based on common descent as opposed to the term caste which is applied to a social unit founded on common occupation, common residence, common language or common political control'. The 'foreigners like Ahirs and Gujjars' were identified with the first. It was admitted later that it was difficult to maintain the distinction between the two as they were 'different ways of looking at the same social groups, the tribe being the forerunner of the caste' (Enthoven, 1975). The notion of common descent existed among tribes and castes.There were also complications connected with occupation, domicile and religion, and hybridization and mixing up of populations. The colonial ethnographers supported by their Indian colleagues explored the foreign elements in the Maharashtrian population. The survey also dealt with hypergamy across peoples (the Abyssinian–Maratha, Koli chiefs–Maratha), and across castes and sub-castes. There was also theorizing about fissioning of people into castes and occupation groups, like among the Brahmanas and baniyas of Gujarat who shared surnames and other traits, following inter alia a change of domicile which created new sub-castes.

Following the reorganization of states in 1956, Berar which had been ethnographically studied as part of the Central Provinces by Russell and Hiralal, and the five districts of Marathwada which were studied by Siraj-ul Hasan (1923) as part of the Nizam's dominion (Osmanabad, Bid, Aurangabad, Parsam, and Nanded), were transferred to Maharashtra. The reconstituted Maharashtra was studied for the first time under the People of India project.

The territory now represented by the Central Provinces and Berar was covered in the colonial period by the ethnographic survey launched under the aegis of the Ethnographic Survey of India, 1901–08. The survey was conducted by administrators as elsewhere. H.V. Russell was the census superintendent, and Hiralal was his assistant. The latters' career illustrates the transformation of a colonial administrator into an ethnographer and a historian. In his book, Russell pays tribute to 'the most loyal and unselfish aid' extended by Hiralal in personally collecting a large part of the original information for the volumes. He further tells us:

The work for the Central Provinces was entrusted to the author, and its preparation, undertaken in addition to ordinary official duties, has been spread over a number of years. The prescribed plan was that a separate account should be written of each of the principal tribe[s] and castes, according to the method adopted in Sir Herbert Risley's *Tribes and Castes of Bengal*. This was considered to be desirable as the book is *intended primarily as a work of reference for the officers of Government who may desire to know something of the customs of the people among whom their work lies*. It has the disadvantage of involving a *large amount of repetition of the same or* very similar statements about different castes, and the result is likely therefore to be somewhat *distasteful to the ordinary reader*. On the other hand, there is no doubt that this method of treatment, if conscientiously followed out, will produce more exhaustive result[s] than a general account.

(Russell and Hiralal, 1918; emphasis added)

The ethnographic survey of tribes and castes of the Central Provinces, conducted by Russell and Hiralal, was thus undertaken in terms of the format of the ethnographic survey laid down by H.H. Risley as early as in 1885. This format was designed to generate information on a few parameters, not all, of the life, occupation, and culture of a community. They related to the origin of the castes, and structure of castes and sub-castes, marriage, other life-cycle ceremonies, religion, occupation, and status. In case of the larger communities such as the Gonds, the canvas was stretched to include many other aspects of life and culture. In fact, there was an unevenness, a measure of inequality, in the description of various communities. None of the works of colonial ethnography of this region discusses methodology. But it is presumed, and the involvement of an official like Hiralal suggests, that information was collected from local revenue officials like the *patwari*s and the tehsildars, school teachers and local headmen who could be relied upon to provide authentic information. It should also be noted that the ethnographic survey was conducted as a follow up to the 1901 census operation. By this time a distinction had already been made between tribe and caste, a tribe being a backward, remotely situated, relatively distant community which had not been absorbed by caste societies.

Risley, like other ethnographers steeped in the Orientalist traditions, had been influenced by the textual notions of Indian society. They appear to have borrowed their entire schema of varna, mixed or hybrid jatis, notion of purity and pollution, from the Sanskrit texts, which were foisted upon the communities in the course of the survey. These ethnographers were also fascinated, even bewildered, by the multiplicity of religions and sects, and the prevalence of magic, witchcraft, and superstitions of all kinds. A list of the anthropological texts cited by Russell in his foreword suggests the extent of his reliance on the works of Frazer and other contemporaries.

One of the interesting features of the ethnography of this period was the mixing of the so-called Dravidian categories of language and caste. Ethnographic texts like those of Russell and Hiralal describe the Dravidian both as a language and a caste category. This serious error committed by Risley was discovered much later, but much harm had been done by then. It was part of the much larger myth of the Aryan as a race pitted against the Dravidian, another race. In fact, the Aryans and the Dravidians did not represent racial categories. There does not seem to be any evidence of racial conflict either. They represent language families which interacted a great deal.

The ethnographic survey was extended to provinces such as Sind. A few princely states such as Mysore, Travancore–Cochin, Baroda, and Hyderabad also participated in the survey.

The census and ethnographic survey had a major impact on indigenous writing. People started using terms like jati, purana, and *vansawali*. For example, there is considerable ethnographic literature in Hindi and its local variants. We examined a numberof jati Puranas kept at the library of Nagari Pracharni Sabha in Varanasi, and were told about the Chanwar Purana of the Chamar community, which we did not manage to see. The format of Jati Purana is similar to one another. They deal with the high status of the communities in the past, their degradation, the need for social reform, education, and mobilization, largely in terms of Sanskritization.

A major survey was launched by G.H. Desai resulting in the publication of *A Glossary of Castes, Tribes and Races in Baroda State* (1912) which is rated as a more competent study than the official report by Enthoven on the Bombay presidency. Nagendra Nath Basu produced eight volumes of ethnography in Bengali on castes and sects of Bengal under the title *Banger Jatio Itihas* (1936). According to the scholars who read the book, it is based on the genealogies (*panji*s) maintained by the genealogists (*panjikar*s), and Basu's considerable field work. The description of the castes and sects are said to be more extensive and more authentic than the report by Risley.

6

Ethnography and Census

As mentioned earlier, the census and ethnographic ventures originated in the colonial need for information about people to facilitate governance and to expedite the exploitation of their skills and resources. Both were thus linked by common objectives and manned by the same administrative cadre which planned and operated the census and ethnographic surveys, and analysed and wrote out the materials generated by these gigantic bureaucratic operations on caste and tribe, their classification/categorization, occupation, ranking, and so on. At the highest level colonial administrators like E.A. Gait, H.H. Risley, and J.H. Hutton spanned the census and ethnographic surveys and the studies undertaken by them later. In the provinces colonial officers like Russell and Hiralal continued the same traditions of participating in the census and conducting ethnographic surveys. Multiple examples of this kind may be found particularly at the district level where the officers participated in the census and wrote ethnographic notes on castes and tribes in their area, and then went on to write settlementary reports and also helped in writing gazetteers, both of which contained a good deal of ethnographic materials.

The census of 1881 was the most complex—or the 'most chaotic'—of all the censuses in the colonial period. It generated a list of 11,645 castes, sub-castes, and so on, which was later found to be too large to be true. However, this unprecedented churning of the Indian populations led to a creative upsurge. Jati Puranas were written on a larger scale than before. Three colonial census/ethnographer officials, namely. H.H. Risley, Denzil C.J. Ibbetson, and J.C. Nesfield—two of whom were to distinguish themselves in both census and ethnography—met to draw up a twenty-seven-point format of the ethnographic survey of British India, which held the ground for the next sixty years (1885–1945). Caste was explored in all its aspects and down to its irreducible units. Caste was defined, and later tribe was defined in relation to caste in the census of 1901. The notion of tribe evolved through the censuses till the label of primitive tribe was replaced by that of the scheduled tribes in 1936. The notion of ranking of castes was introduced. A scramble for placement ensued. A 'pestiferous deluge' of claims and counterclaims occurred. The ethnographic aspect of the census was considered too problematic, and was as good as given up in 1941, even before the colonial period came to a close in 1947.

However, the colonial census did generate an enormous amount of data on castes/tribes, religions, occupations, language, and even on such minor ethnographic aspects as place names. Some of the census officials who moved into the area of ethnographic studies were also Orientalists steeped in textual notions of Indian society. They were also exposed to the dominant colonial ideology that extolled the superiority of the white race. And yet it should be noted that there was a thin line dividing census and ethnography. The census did not count all castes. There was a cut-off point, minor castes/tribes were left out, but ethnographers studied almost all communities.

A crucial aspect of census ethnography has been the listing of communities. In fact, listing of communities has been problematic, not so much in regard the very upper crust or the lowest stratum, which have been identified with a fair measure of consistency. It has been problematic with regard to the vast middle space where communities have been discarding old names and assuming new names in search of a new identity. The listing of communities started in 1806 in the Madras presidency in the pre-census phase in which both varna and jati categories were mixed up. In Sanskrit texts, as also in popular parlance, varna and jati are interchangeable. It was the census of 1881, which, as mentioned earlier, produced the largest list of castes, which consists of phonetic variations of the castes of Tamil, Telugu, Canerese, and Malayalam, all linguistic categories, and a list of castes from other parts of India. Risley's estimate of the number of castes based on the 1881 census hovered around 2,000. The first authentic list of communities was produced by the census of 1931, which in many respects also produced the most authentic ethnographic material. The People of India (PoI) project puts the number of communities at 2,204 with about 580 segments, making a total of 2,800 communities/ segments. Unlike the census, the PoI covered all communities but did not categorize them.

It was puzzling that none of the lists of caste produced by the census over the period of sixty years from 1881 to 1941 were exactly similar. In fact, establishing equivalence has been a major exercise.

Three points of interest emerge from this discussion. The first is that the total number of communities/subgroups oscillate around 3,000 mark. Second, the substantial number of communities is common to the census lists (1881–1941). The third and final point of interest is that the census lists of communities and the PoI list of communities are not exactly similar, and that the measure of equivalence with the PoI list of communities increases with successive censuses. For instance, the 1931 census list of communities is closest to the PoI list in term of similarities, while the 1881 census is farthest removed in term of comparison.

In fact, both colonial censuses and ethnographic surveys tried to present a comprehensive profile of the Indian populations, covering ethnographic or social, linguistic, and biological dimensions.

This particularly needs to be discussed with reference to the census of 1931. The census report of 1931 was easily the most comprehensive of all such reports, complete with maps, statistics, ethnographic accounts, and the provinces' reports, together with a three-volume all-India report. It was rightly regarded as representing the summit of the series of the census reports that began to be filed from 1881 in the colonial period (K.S. Singh, introduction in 1986 edn of *Census of India* [*CoI* hereafter] 1931: I).

A merit of this report is that it gives, for the first time, a reasonably accurate estimate of the number and distribution of primitive tribes. As Hutton (CoI, 1931) says, no serious attempt had been made from 1891 onwards to arrive at the figures of the hill and forest tribes. The 1891 figure of fifteen million was incomplete. The 1921 data of sixteen million omitted not only many major tribes but also many small ones. In contrast, the 1931 census enumerated all primitive tribes (142 in all).

Similarly, this report contained the first authentic description of all the exterior castes now labelled as the scheduled castes. This nomenclature represented a transition from the concept of the depressed classes in the previous censuses which was considered derogatory, to the term exterior which connoted 'exclusion but not extrusion'. In pursuance of the official policy to generate a better knowledge of the backward and depressed classes and of the problems involved in their present and future welfare, the 1931 census prepared a complete list of the castes that suffered from social disabilities, such as denial of access to temples, schools, and wells, particularly in the south. The definition of this category was made more rigorous by the inclusion of such parameters as servicing or non-servicing by Brahmanas, barbers, water carriers, and tailors and pollution by touch and acceptance of water. The 1921 census had estimated the minimum number of the depressed castes at 52.6 million as against 42 million given by the Franchise Committee of 1919. The 1931 census actually identified 277 castes together with the tea garden codie castes and others (like Sudra, Valmiki, Ramdasia,) adding up to a population of 50,195,77 (CoI, 1931). The exterior caste was replaced by the scheduled caste in 1936.

Contrary to general impression, the census of 1931 did not generate data on all castes, which could be and is supposed to be used by caste lobbies particularly during elections today. In fact, the scope of this census in regard to the coverage of castes was rather restricted. The state census officials were told not to tabulate figures for such castes as the state government did not approve of, and the minimum of four rather than two per mille (191) was suggested as the minimal demographic standard for enumeration of a dozen or so of the selected castes of wide distribution.

All census officials were fascinated by primitive religion and the process of its absorption into Hinduism. Unlike others, however, Hutton used his formidable scholarship to identify such elements of the tribal material being absorbed into Hinduism as unmistakably bore the impact of primitive religion.

Hutton's racial classification of the Indian population was based on B.S. Guha's report which he described as 'easily the most important contribution to the physical anthropology of India since Risley's survey'. In fact, the third part of the report on the census of India, 1931 puts together within the framework of an ethnographical report B.S. Guha's report on the racial affinities of the peoples of India (Guha in *CoI*, 1931: III [A], see 1986 edn), as also the ethnographic notes by various scholars. Study of the physical characteristics and language of the people of India started as part of colonial ethnography. The first systematic study of the classification of Indian races was undertaken by Herbert Risley in 1901. In spite of its many lacunae it was regarded as a landmark in the study ofthe people of India. Both Hutton and Guha identified the gaps in Risley's study. Based on such a critique of Risley's work, Guha's survey, taken up as part of the census operation, was comparatively a professionally competent and comprehensive exercise. Measurements were taken on eighteen different characters with standard instruments; 3,374 persons in all, belonging to fifty-one 'racial' groups, were measured mostly by Guha himself. The total number of communities which Guha examined was fifty-one, out of which thirty-four were examined before the census. They included the Brahmanas, caste Hindus, and aborigines, both male and female.

The second part of this report consists of the results of findings of a short, quick ethnographic survey of communities, mostly tribals, which was undertaken as part of the census operation of 1931. Before this, Risley in 1901 had put together material on physical and cultural anthropology of various castes and tribes in the ethnographic appendix to his report of the census of 1901. Hutton tried to generate his material systematically in terms of an eighteen-point format which dealt with division into clans and groups, traditions of origin, material culture, folklore, system of belief, mode of making fire, and so on.

The 1941 census was a relatively modest affair, with data presented for a limited number of communities at the district level, such as the scheduled castes (sixty-two in all), scheduled tribes (fourteen), and other castes (fifty-six).

The post-colonial phase has witnessed the breakdown of the nexus of census and ethnography. No enumeration of caste has been taken up since the 1951 census, as caste tends to be divisive. All ethnographic studies connected with census and resulting from census have been discontinued. The focus is now on economic and demographic parameters. Only the scheduled castes and scheduled tribes continue to be enumerated and studied. The 1961 census produced a number of monographs based on socio-economic surveys of about 500 villages in the country, and materials based on urban surveys, and dealing with traditional crafts and fairs and festivals. Ethnographic survey of all other communities has been a taboo.

The point to be considered is whether there is a need for a detailed ethnographic survey in the vastly changed post-Mandal context. With the judgement of the Supreme Court delivered in the reservation matter, caste has come back to the centre of administration and political power, where it always was but was not as explicitly recognized. The Supreme Court has also directed the Government of India and state governments to siphon off the creamy layers of the other backward classes by introducing the economic criterion. It appears that the Supreme Court has largely gone by the experiences of Karnataka which initiated pioneering measures, with experiences of reservation going back to the turn of the century (in Mysore), in identifying the more eligible categories of backward sections of the people who should get the benefits of reservation. Two experiments of Karnataka are worth mentioning in this regard. One was the first-hand household socio-economic backwardness, and both economic and educational backwardness. This second part of the work, associated with the commission led by Chinnappa Reddy, was described as a model by the Government of India in the debate on the Mandal Commission. The reason for mentioning the Karnataka experience is that we cannot avoid the survey of backward classes and this may be considered necessary by the census in 2011.

A detailed ethnographic survey has already been carried out by the Anthropological Survey of India under the PoI project, which should facilitate the enumeration of the communities in terms of socio-economic criteria of backwardness. There is no need to shy away from such enumeration of all communities including a large number of backward classes, particularly of the weaker segments of the backward classes. The PoI project is already generating the data on scheduled castes, scheduled tribes, and minorities in terms of some of the socioeconomic parameters. With the consistent application of the economic criteria, the 'pejorative' nature of caste may dwindle and the fear of its divisiveness, which has prevented enumeration of castes since the census of 1931, should disappear.

7

Anthropological Survey of India
A Historical Perspective*

The first question that is always asked about the establishment of the Anthropological Survey of India is why the colonial authorities were in such a tearing hurry to set up this organization before their departure. This survey was the last of the survey organizations to be established, starting from the Survey of India, Geological Survey of India, Botanical Survey of India, and Zoological Survey of India, formed by the colonial regime to map out the resources of the country for the benefit of British capital and for good governance, as W.W. Hunter (1877) puts it. The Anthropological Survey of India (ASI) was set up in December 1945, barely twenty months before the transfer of power took place. The reason for this has to be sought in the intensive lobbying done by the administrator–anthropologists over the previous fifteen years to create a special dispensation for the tribes under the Government of India Act of 1935, and through various suggestions and proposals including those for the creation of the Crown Colony in the North East and a protectorate for the tribals. They include J.P. Mills, J.H. Hutton,

* First published in 2000 as 'A Perspective on the ASI', *Seminar*, no. 495, November. Copyright Seminar Publications.

W. Grigson, W.G. Archer, and others, with anthropologists like Verrier Elwin and C. Von Furer-Haimendorf lending support. Their special interest in the tribes derived from a romantic tradition that presented the tribals in pleasant contrast to castes, the free spirit of the hill people, the 'unravished' hills and plateaus where they lived that reminded the colonial rulers of their homeland, and from their appreciation of the strategic location of the tribes and the enormous resources that their land contained. However, these proposals were shot down by the Home Office which felt that after the Second World War England would be too impoverished to commit its meagre resources to such ventures.

But the proposal to establish an anthropological survey to study the tribal people was pursued despite financial constraints. The reason for this was the single-minded pursuit of the idea by Dr B.S. Guha who headed the anthropological unit located in the Zoological Survey of India from 1927. Guha moved at two levels. First, he got a formal memorandum on the creation of the Anthropological Survey of India submitted by the Zoological Survey of India, and pursued the matter officially with the support of his bosses and J.H. Hutton with whom he had worked. Hutton was the census commissioner of the 1931 census, and Guha had compiled the third part of the ethnographic notes which appeared with the all-India Reports. Hutton had retired and become a professor of Anthropology at Cambridge. Guha kept him dutifully informed of the developments. In fact, there was a very interesting interaction of ideas (K.S. Singh, 1994a) on the formation of the ASI. Academics like S.C. Roy and others emphasized the need for recognition of anthropology as a science. These academics and administrator–academics like R.B. Seymour Sewell, formerly director, Zoological Survey of India, argued for the establishment of the Anthropological Survey of India as an independent organization which could be part of the scheme for post-war reconstruction. Sewell stated forcefully in his letter dated 19 March 1945 that an independent India would require the creation of a scientific survey to have a full knowledge of the races that include some of the most cultured as well as others of the most primitive form of civilization who should be protected. The preservation of the social and cultural characteristics of various races, and especially of the aboriginal tribes, was of great importance, he added. At the second level, Guha approached Verrier Elwin who had broken with the Congress and become influential in the British official circles (Ramachandra Guha, 1999). Both admired each other. Elwin wrote to the governor of the Central Provinces, Sir Francis Wylie, formally suggesting the appointment of a scientific advisor on aboriginal problems. A portion of his letter dated 8 November 1944 bears reproduction:

As usual the chief difficulty would be the man, for India is not rich in anthropologists. But there is at least one man[,] perhaps the only man[,] who would fill such a post with the necessary distinction and authority. He is B.S. Guha who is indisputably the mot eminent of our Anthropologists and has the advantage of being both a biologist and a sociologist. He has been formerly 20 years in the Zoological Survey of India; in the 1932 census, when he was Hutton's Assistant, he became familiar with tribesmen in every part of India; most useful of all, he has had experience of how the Americans handle their problem, for he was engaged by Smithsonian institution in the Indian Ereservations of Coloroda and New Mexico. He is a Hindu, but not too much of one, and his scientific integrality as well as his administrative ability is beyond question. (K.S. Singh, 1994a)

Elwin pursued the matter in his editorial in the journal *Man in India*:

In the judgment of Man in India the time has come for the Government of India to establish a separate Anthropological Survey of India as part of its scheme for post-war reconstruction. The most grandiose plans for scientific research are being considered. Every aspect of man's material environment is to be investigated: only Man himself is being ignored. Yet the lesson of history is emphatic; an exclusive emphasis on the physical sciences and neglect of social, psychological and moral side of human life ends only in destruction. In India, both for the credit of the science and for the well-being of the population—especially of the tribal population—the establishment of the Anthropological Survey is an urgent necessity. (Elwin, 1945)

However, this proposal seems to have been rejected at the beginning because of opposition from some officials who did not want an 'anthropological dictator' to interfere in the tribal affairs which the missionaries with the backing of an official lobby had been left free to manage. The 'Anglicized' Guha was considered too good a Hindu to be trusted with the job. However, neither Guha nor Elwin gave up. They continued to build pressure. Guha proposed Elwin as deputy director. One does not know whether Elwin's endeavours had any effect. The formal proposal sent through the official channels however produced results.

The ASI was created in December 1945 and located temporarily in Benaras. It was a small organization to begin with. Guha and Elwin became the first director and deputy director respectively. Guha also acted as the anthropological advisor to the Government of India, Elwin's equivalent of a scientific advisor on aboriginal problems. From this small but serious beginning, the Anthropological Survey of India (ASI), which was later shifted to Calcutta, grew into the biggest organization of this kind in the world, with the largest number of professional anthropologists and scholars of allied disciplines working under one roof. Guha built on the concept of anthropology as a unified discipline, combining physical anthropology and cultural anthropology with inputs provided by various allied disciplines such as psychology, ecology, folklore, and biochemistry. This structure has by and large endured. However, some of the colonial trappings have remained. A number of 'stations' were set up during the period 1951–76. Inter-disciplinary 'expeditions' were sent out to 'discover' or 'find' people and study them, in Andaman and Nicobar Islands, Arunachal Pradesh (formerly North-east Frontier Agency), Nagaland, Central Himalayas, Kerala, and other regions. One such expedition to Rupkund almost cost Guha's successor, N. Datta Majumdar, his job! The projects of research were generally sporadic, local, and specific and related largely to the study of the tribal people which was also the main concern of colonial anthropology. Other subjects included culture areas, culture traits, religious centres and institutions, nomads, fisher folk, slum dwellers, and minorities. The allied sections undertook research in osteologcal studies of historic and pre-historic human remains, tribal languages carrying capacity of land, and so on.

The decolonization of the ASI was speeded up during the 1960s with projects of national dimensions being taken up. The Ethno-graphic Survey of India, undertaken by the colonial regime in 1901, was basically 'provincial' in its area of operation even though it was generally guided by an all-India format. While it covered most of British India, only a few princely states took up the survey. The Ethnographic Survey of India (1905–09) also suffered from lack of financial resources. In striking contrast with this, the Anthropological Survey of India launched the first All-India Survey of Material Culture and the All-India Anthropological Survey of Populations. This presented a major breakthrough not only in terms of conceptual framework but also in terms of methodology. The quick, short-term methodology of field work was introduced for the first time, for the first survey had resulted in the generation of an enormous amount of data on material culture including crafts, occupation, food habits, and toilet practices. Unfortunately, most of these data remained unpublished until much later.

While a small number of area/regional studies were undertaken, the ASI remained occupied with micro-level studies mostly concentrated at one or two places. Therefore, a massive reorganization of the ASI was undertaken from the mid 1970s. This aimed at decentralization and devolution of power and functions, making regional stations—redesignated as offices and later as centres—autonomous so that they could take up both regional and all-India projects with speed and efficiency. Projects were distributed all over the country within the framework of regional and all-India studies. Coordination was sought to be established with the university departments of anthropology and research centres in order to promote exchange of ideas and experiences in the field of anthropology. More of all-India projects were designed in order to generate an all-India profile of people and society. In the first phase, surveys of tribal movements, tribal economies, and tribal customary laws were taken up to generate the all-India profile. In all these projects, the methodology of short-term, quick survey focused on specific issues was further developed and refined. A survey of linguistic traits was also undertaken.

In 1976 the ASI was entrusted with the task of designing the first museum of anthropology. With this it remained involved for almost twelve years, from 1976 to 1988. Both anthropology and the anthropological museum, which was known as the Museum of Man, were located in zoology departments that stressed the 'genetical' relationship between zoology and anthropology. The early concerns were primarily with the evolution of man, and other linked areas. However, in the post-colonial period, the focus shifted to other concerns such as biological variation, evolution of culture and civilization, and cultural pluralism, identity, ethnicity, and interaction as new areas of interest. Therefore, the first outline of the National Museum of Anthropology brought out by the ASI in 1977 sought to bring together the perspectives on these subjects generated by physical anthropology, archaeology, and cultural anthropology. The project was revised in 1982 to stress on conceptu-alization, the linkages with environment, technology, and culture. The museum was not going to be either a tribal museum, though tribes would occupy an important place, nor an ethnographical museum, but a museum that would combine both the universal and national perspectives on biological variation and cultural diversities. The ASI remained closely associated with the establishment of the Rashtriya Manav Sangrahalaya in recognition of the ASI's pioneering contribu-tions to its formation. From 1988 onwards, the museum has further developed, setting in motion a museum movement and fleshing out various dimensions of the original and enlarged concepts.

This formed the background to the People of India (PoI) project launched in 1985, in terms of the parameters of a rapidly emerging post-colonial ethnography extending beyond the territorial limits of co-lonial ethnography. For the first time, the PoI project undertook the survey of the human surface of the entire country. Keeping in mind the provisions of the constitution of India and the human groups, such as the Scheduled Castes, Scheduled Tribes, and Other Backward Classes, and the linguistic and religious minorities that it identifies for special treatment, the project also noted the provisions of equality and social justice that had to be translated in terms of equal treatment of all people in the survey and anthropological studies.

Although no policy resolution had been adopted by the Anthropological Survey of India in this early phase, committing it to the study of tribals only, in fact anthropology, particularly cultural anthropology, remained concerned largely with the study of tribals, just as sociology was concerned with caste. Therefore, to make matters explicit, the policy resolution was drastically revised in 1985 to commit the organization to the survey of all the people of India, both tribes and non-tribes. The PoI project also sought to survey the people in cultural, linguistic, and biological dimensions. It generated for the first time data on languages and adscript used within the community and for inter-community communication, for all groups including those which were barred by the census for reason of their smallness. Unlike Risley's ethnographic survey, the PoI project did not generate first-hand anthropometric data but drew on its earlier surveys and studies to cover the biological dimension. In short, it sought to present a composite bio-linguistic cultural profile of all communities of India. The concerns of environment, resource use, gender relations, impact of change and development, market and technology were appropriately reflected in a fifteen-point format which was uniformly canvassed for all groups. The project also involved the updating and publication of the old data sets generated by all-India projects of the 1960s. While the continuity of the ethnographic tradition was stressed by using the previously gathered information as the benchmark, the focus of the PoI project was on change.

The methodology of quick, short-term survey undertaken by scholars who were familiar with the terrain was further developed. The objective was to profile all communities of India, the impact of change and their development process, and the linkages that bring them together. These short, descriptive profiles would add up to the first ever national ethnographic profile of the people of India, going far beyond the exercise attemptsof the colonial censuses from 1881 to 1931. Computer technology was used to generate and store information. For the first time, ethnographic software was produced. This massive exercise spread over fifteen years resulted in a forty-three-volume output running into 40,000 pages. In all, 4,694 communities were identified. Most of them concentrated in eco-cultural zones within the states. In fact, the communities could best be seen in relationship to environment, language, and regional/local culture. It was also noticed that the communities shared a good many traits such as language, folklore, elements of material culture, custom, dress and ornaments, cuisine, and so on. This project has therefore been described as an exploration of diversities and linkages or affinities among the people of India.

While an enormous range of information and knowledge generated by the PoI project has been appreciated and absorbed in various ways, there has been the criticism that it is a piece of 'bureaucratic gigantism'. The census is given as another example. In fact, the Anthropological Survey of India like other survey organization has been criticized for peddling *sarkari* stuff. All survey organizations, whether as subordinate or autonomous organizations, have been structurally part of the government and of the concerned departments and ministries. They are closely tied up with the policies and programmes of the government as laid down from time to time in the policy documents and in the plans. But there is also considerable autonomy in matters of research, planning, and operations. It is not correct to say that it is sarkari anthropology all the way.

Major projects have been taken up by the directors which have reflected their concerns. They have been left free to operationalize their projects. The PoI project, both in its conceptual framework and in its methodology, represented a continuing tradition and also a very major advance in terms of the magnitude of operations, perceptions, and insights that it generated. The ASI has also the anthropological advisor to the Government of India. The close interaction that was made possible with various departments of the Government of India with research institutions located in Delhi, and with scholars and institutions from all over the country, was because of easy communication from the capital. This was reflected in the number of cultural projects formulated by the ASI and taken up by the Department of Culture for implementation, like the rapid organization of the Rashtriya Manav Sangrahalaya as mentioned earlier, or the involvement of the Survey in conflict resolution processes whether in Bodoland or in Jharkhand. The inputs provided by the Survey related to the safeguard of identity, language, and culture, and the formation of autonomous bodies within the framework of the existing state governments. In the case of Jharkhand, the autonomous body was supposed to be the first step towards the formation of the state. Unfortunately, the autonomy model collapsed and the movement for formation of a state surged ahead.

A major initiative taken by the ASI also related to the survival of the endangered Negrito groups in the Andaman and Nicobar Islands. The proposal to establish a bridgehead in the Jarawa territory was resisted firmly so that the Jarawas did not meet the fate of the Onges and the Great Andamanese. Unfortunately however, the Jarawas have now started arriving in Port Blair town which is likely to have consequences that one shudders to imagine!

To sum up, anthropology as a discipline is developing very rapidly all over the world, branching out into new areas—there are as many as 120 sub-disciplines—and opening up exciting possibilities all round. The impact of the developments in human genetics, particularly through human genome projects for health, is one such area. Anthropology is also becoming popular as a subject for students and general readers. For a country of such diversity like India, anthropology will continue to remain popular: in fact, it will become more and more popular. The task of generating a composite profile of all population groups of India which cover biological, linguistic, and cultural dimensions, and of updating the database presented in the PoI project will be the one of the major challenges of the twenty-first century. Therefore, attention needs to be paid to two tasks. The first is about enlarging the area of research and upgrading its quality in close coordination with the departments of Anthropology and related research organizations, training of scholars and their exposure to new developments in their field. The 1881 census had a strong impact in generating ethnographic accounts, jati Puranas, etc. A considerable ethnographic literature emerged in Gujarati, Bengali, Tamil, some of which were even rated better than the official ethnographic accounts. Currently, there are sporadic attempts at writing anthropology in local/regional languages. However, concerted and well-directed efforts are still required to generate first-hand material in anthropology in all languages of India, which will make it a truly vibrant discipline for people.

8

The People of India
Diversities and Affinities

Over the last twelve years the Anthropological Survey of India (ASI) has been engaged in generating, retrieving, compiling, and analysing a vast amount of data on the human heritage of India. In 1984, fresh initiatives were taken to retrieve, compile, and analyse the data on the anthropometric survey of India undertaken in the 1960s (Basu and Sreenath, 1995, 1996a and b) and the dataset yielded by the All-India Bio-anthropological Survey initiated in the 1970s (Ghosh, 1988). The two datasheets have already been published in many volumes, and the remaining volumes are likely to be published in a couple of years. Similarly, the data on the survey of linguistic traits, undertaken in the 1970s, has been published (Krishan, 1990).

Against this background the ASI launched the People of India (PoI) project on 2 October 1985 with a view to generating a brief, descriptive anthropological profile of all communities of India, the impact on them of change and development, and the linkages between them. The format, both structured and open-ended, had four parts. The first related to the ethno-origin and distribution of communities and their self-perception, the second dealt with social organization of the community, the third with economy and the impact of change and development, and the fourth and last one explored the linkages, both traditional and modern, among communities. Ethnography has a continuing tradition. However, in colonial times, ethnographic communities were primarily studied as islands. The post-colonial ethnography explores the linkages and relationships of the communities engaged in the task of nation building on multi-ethnic and multi-cultural societies. The honeycomb model of interaction was suggested for such societies in which communities are engaged in the process of vibrant interaction.

THE LOGISTICS

Over almost a decade following the launching of the project, it has been possible to identify and locate the study of 4,694 communities in all states/union territories of India, and computerize the data for this large number of communities. Yet, in spite of all efforts to identify all communities, there still remains a grey area, though a small one, where identities are still fluid and identification problematic. The communities thus identified included the Scheduled Tribes (461), Scheduled Castes (445), and other communities. The transfer of the data to computers started at an early stage in March 1988, and for the first time in the country a software was developed on ethnography, which was also probably among the first of its kind in the world. This was a vast project in which not only scholars from all parts of India and at all levels participated, but also common people and local scholars who not only generated information but also wrote out the material. Therefore, at one stage this project was described as one on the people of India by the people of India. Four hundred and seventy scholars participated in it including 245 from outside the ASI. Twenty-six institutions other than the ASI were involved as well. About 120 workshops and rounds of discussions were held in all states/union territories in which about 2,000 scholars participated to plan the studies and evaluate the findings. The investigators spent 24,880 days in the field and interviewed 21,536 people, of whom 5,353 were women, in villages (4,513), mostly multi-community villages, and in towns (941) spread over most of the districts (438) and eco-cultural regions as identified under the project. The states were further divided into about ninety-six natural eco-cultural zones defined by dialect, folklore, history, administration, and so on. About 21,362 photographs covering 2,548 communities were generated to build up the visual documentation of the people of India. A large number of maps showing the distribution of the communities were also prepared.

The project was entirely *swadeshi*, or homespun. All knowledge is both universal and specific, and anthropology as a branch of knowledge is closely related to culture and environment. In this discipline every culture is unique, and so is every trait. This project also sought to explore the idioms, the structures, and the cognitive processes reflected in the understanding and perception of people about themselves, and their relationship to one another and with the environment.

The above surveys covering biological, linguistic, and cultural dimensions which have evolved in tandem seek to generate a composite profile of all the people of India. Each community is covered in terms of biological variation, linguistic traits, and cultural and socio-cultural aspects. The output is enormous. Out of the forty-three-volume PoI project, twelve volumes have already been published and the remaining are to be published over the next two to three years. Thus, by the end of the century we should have a large corpus of materials running into about a hundred volumes covering the biological, linguistic, and cultural profiles of the people of India.

It is interesting to note that the explosion of so much information—and so much knowledge—about people has coincided with similar developments at the international level. In fact, in no other period of human history has so much information and so much knowledge been generated and disseminated about people and about diversities. With this knowledge of diversities, a new notion of community—or the old notion reinforced by current concerns—has emerged. This is the notion of community rooted in its environment, its resources, and in various networks of relationships. The environmental movements, the movement of the indigenous people, the ethnic explosion, and many other developments have tended to converge and reinforce the notion of community, irrespective of labels, as something far more basic in its formation than we have understood so far.

Yet another development has been an attempt to establish linkages where they exist among diversities of all kinds. There is a wide range of information today on biodiversity, which is now being linked up with linguistic and cultural diversities. In fact, all three dimensions are closely related, each reinforcing the others.

The people of India derive their identity from India, that is, Bharat. The notion of Bharat which has evolved came to be applied to the landmass lying south of the Himalayas, bounded by the oceans. The authors of the Puranas have written about this territorial configuration. Poets from Kalidasa to Rabindranath Tagore and Subramanya Bharti have eulogized it. It was in the course of the freedom struggle that this territorial identity was fused with deep emotion, as compositions glorifying the land and seeking freedom for it—usually described as 'Mata' or 'Bharat mata'—poured out in various languages. Jawaharlal Nehru declared that 'Bharat mata' was the people of India.

BIOLOGICAL DIVERSITY OF THE PEOPLE

DNA-based studies should tell us finally about the pattern of the peopling of the subcontinent. All that is known for definite at this stage is that the Homo sapiens sapiens originated in eastern Africa from where they migrated in waves upon waves to different parts of the world including our own. According to present estimates, Australia was peopled about 40,000 BC and the Americas around 15,000 BC by the Caucasoid. Even without going so much into prehistory, it could be mentioned that different communities of India recall their recent or not-so-recent migration in their oral traditions, jati Puranas, and history. Migrations have varied in range. An Indian is a migrant par excellence. Communities have settled in different ecological and climatic regions of India and derived their identity from hills and valleys, the plains, islands, and villages, particularly the ancestral villages.

The communities are rather unevenly distributed across states and union territories. By far the largest numbers of communities (above 350) are in Andhra Pradesh and Tamil Nadu. They vary between 250 and 350 in Uttar Pradesh, Bihar, Madhya Pradesh, Maharashtra,

Orissa, Karnataka, and Gujarat. The range varies from 150 to 250 communities in West Bengal, Rajasthan, and Kerala. Arunachal Pradesh, Assam, Tripura, Jammu and Kashmir, Himachal Pradesh, Haryana, and Punjab have communities ranging from 15 to 150. The number of communities drops to below fifty in Nagaland, Manipur, Mizoram, Meghalaya, Sikkim, Goa, Chandigarh, and the Bay islands. Each state/union territory has been treated as a unit of our study. The various stated regions of India are not only politico-administrative units, they are also linguistic units and ethnic units because most communities (72 per cent) are located within each one of them. Only a few (about 24 per cent) are distributed over adjoining areas, and about 4 per cent are distributed over a larger part of the country.

Probably nowhere in the world has there existed so many communities—4,694 including the main communities (2,205), major segments (589), and territorial units (1,900). These communities have been identifying themselves in various ways through history, by territory, by varna and jati, by occupation, and so on. In addition to the names or nomenclatures of communities, there is an impressive range of synonyms, surnames, and titles. No community is without divisions, and there are a large number of segments.

LINGUISTIC DIVERSITY

The diversities in terms of linguistic traits are wide ranging. There are as many as 325 languages divided into five language families. Twenty-five scripts are in use. The linguistic situation is because Indians have a natural ease with language and most of them speak a number of languages, or at least two. And yet it is fascinating that many linguistic traits have penetrated across the five language families. India has been variously described as a socio-linguistic area, a single semantic area, a single linguistic and cultural unit. In the language contact situations, the incidence of bilingualism is rather much too conservative (13 per cent estimated in 1981). One of the reasons for this could be mother tongue loyalty. Some tribals are trilingual. No state in India is unilingual in spite of the preponderance of the speakers of the state language.

Most Indians have been a highly mixed people from the early periods of prehistory or history. The skeletal remains at the rock shelter site in Mirzapur dating back to 15,000 BC and those belonging to the Mohenjodaro–Harappa sites suggest the existence of mixed populations. Though racial classification of populations has now been discarded, morphological and genetic variations among populations are being explored; these are present on a larger scale within a community than between communities. There is thus a greater biological diversity among the people of India than among people elsewhere. Yet, at the regional level their likenesses appear to be more than their differences, and the number of genes in which they differ are only a few in comparison with the vast number of common genes. This may be due to the fact that there were waves of migration on a scale larger than probably anywhere else in the world, and that the mating patterns remained relatively flexible for a long period, allowing for a free flow of genes. Caste endogamy emerged in its rigid form at a later period in history. Within a region there was a greater admixture of populations and clustering of traits; there is therefore a much greater homogenization in terms of morphological and genetic traits among communities at the regional level, and most of the communities within a region or state therefore share many traits. This has been brought out significantly in the anthropometrics survey of the populations in various states.

Indians have their own notion of beauty as represented by colour and texture of the skin, which is influenced by the climate. There is a whole range of shades, from fair to dark complexions, described in various evocative terms in classical literature and folklore, existing together. There is a popular saying that a bride should be fair like Sita and a bridegroom should be pleasantly dark like Rama.

Indians are reported to have relatively larger eyes. This may be because our eyes are popping all the time; there is so much beauty, so much diversity to behold!

As mentioned earlier, the communities should be best seen in the context of the ecosystem and eco-cultural zones, as most of them are rooted in their resources. They derive their identity from their environment, and their occupations are based on their resources.

Even the migrant groups seek to assimilate into their new environment except in the matter of the language they speak at home, or in terms of marriage. The rootedness in local eco-cultural systems is an outstanding characteristic of our communities, no matter what religious label is attached to them—Hindu, Muslim, Christian, and so on.

Again, an important feature of our ethnographic scenario has been the range of migration of communities, families, and individuals—most of the communities are migrants—across the length and breadth of the country, their adaptation to local traditions, and their contribution to the development of local traditions, even as or before the 'son of soil' phenomenon emerged.

CULTURAL DIVERSITY

There is also an extraordinary range of diversities in terms of cultural traits, which tend to cluster at various local and regional levels. People cutting across castes and communities share a great deal within an eco-cultural linguistic region or its sub-region. As many as 775 traits have been identified, relating to ecology, settlement, identity, food habits, social organizations, economy and occupation, linkages, and impact of change and development. Within a region, communities cutting across religions share a great many traits. The sharing of traits has to be seen at some other levels also. For example, it appears that a number of states belonging to a linguistic/cultural region share a very high percentage of traits with Muslims (97.7 per cent), Buddhists (91.9 per cent), Sikhs (88.99 per cent), and Jains (77.46 per cent). Other communities which share a high percentage of traits are: Muslim-Sikhs (89.95 per cent), Muslim-Buddhists (91.18 per cent), and Jain-Buddhists (81.34 per cent).

Therefore, the traits we share are far more that the traits that we do not. A reason for sharing of traits on such a large scale could be the fact that most of the communities have emerged from the same ecological, ethnic, and sociocultural background, even though they have later embraced different religions or other ways of life.

FOOD AND DRINK

In spite of the high value attached to vegetarianism, only about 20 per cent of Indian communities are vegetarian. There is vegetarianism of all shades and nuances shaped by the compulsions of ecology, value system, availability of food, and so on. There are vegetarians who take eggs, fertilized or non-fertilized; there are also vegetarians who abstain from onion and avoid garlic. The men are mostly non-vegetarian. A shift from vegetarianism to non-vegetarianism is reported in many communities, and similarly a shift from non-vegetarianism to vegetarianism is also reported but rather weakly, mostly among the Scheduled Castes and Tribes.

With growing affluence, there has also been a sharp increase in the consumption of alcoholic beverages by men. Traditionally, women occasionally consume alcohol in a number of communities. Smoking is very common. Chewing of tobacco and the use of snuff are also widespread. Chewing betel is common in a large number of communities. We are, therefore, largely a drinking, smoking, and meat-eating people.

OCCUPATIONS

As many as twelve major occupations and 307 current occupations, bringing the total to 349, have been identified all over the country. With the diversification of the economy and social mobility, a number of occupations are practised by members within a single jati or community. There are few communities whose members follow only one occupation. The average number of occupations per community stands at 5.3, of which 1.8 is traditional and 3.5 consists of newly acquired occupations. There has been a decline in traditional occupations like hunting, gathering, trapping birds and animals, pastoralism, shifting cultivation, salt-making, and toddy tapping, with the shrinkage of resource base, depletion of forests, and so on. Settled cultivation is the leading occupation, pursued by members of many communities, followed by wage labour and animal husbandry, fishing, and textile weaving. Of modern occupations, government service is the most sought after; members of as many as 3,051 communities reportedly work for the government. Participation is on the increase in business, trade, industrial work, private service, and self-employment sectors.

DISTINCT IDENTITIES

The regions of India have evolved since the prehistoric period into language areas (since the medieval period), and into politico-administrative units as states (twenty-eight) and union territories (seven) today. They have been culturally distinct, the various communities within their ambit sharing a great deal by way of language/dialect, folklore, elements of material culture, customs (*lokachar*s and *desachar*s), local regional dress and ornaments, cuisine, and so on. So strong has been the alchemy of regional identities that those who have gone in have become a part of it. If the matrimonial columns of national dailies are any indication, most people want to marry within their language group.

The Constitution of India, which speaks of the people of India in a collective sense, identifies five groups—the Scheduled Castes, the Scheduled Tribes, the religious and linguistic minorities, the educationally and socially backward classes, and the Anglo-linguistic minorities. All these groups are spread all across the country. Most of them are rooted in their milieu. They have been heterogeneous in terms of their perception of themselves, their differing versions of origin, their kinship structures, their life-cycle ceremonies, their occupations which have now diversified, and so on.

The knowledge thus generated of such formations is two-fold. At one level, a community is projected as homogeneous, marked by the birth and sharing of many elements of culture. At another level, structurally a community is found to be essentially heterogeneous, its members speaking many languages, having different cultural traits, and various morphological and genetic traits, which, as mentioned earlier, are reported to be on a larger scale within a community than between communities.

Indian society is marked by division. There are no communities without divisions. On the face of it, segments (including exogamous divisions, groups, and subgroups), synonyms, surnames, and titles add up to a mind-boggling figure of about 80,000. However, at another level, they form a fascinating tapestry marked by different levels of perception, identity, and status. They also demonstrate a wide range of interaction and sharing, of linkages and commonalities, among communities in a linguistic–regional context.

Each region—and even a few of the sub-regions—has its own cluster of communities, and its own hierarchy of jatis. All communities are placed in a hierarchical order. Based on self-perception and others' perceptions, the communities are now ranked as high, middle, and low. There has been an all-pervasive impact of the development process, even though access to developmental benefits as also to market is rather uneven. As the movement towards political equality grows, and as it is translated into economic terms, there is a swelling of the middle rank. Members of more and more communities from the lower order move into the middle zone. This explains the phenomenon of the burgeoning middle class, an amorphous category which encompasses a whole range of people moving up and down into a growing arena of economic activities. The PoI project highlights the rise of the middle class over a large social spectrum including most communities and from almost all regions. However, there are still some communities which have no adequate representation in these ranks. But even the most remote communities have been down in the vortex of Indian politics, and they are participants in the political process. However, this process has still to move forward so as to encompass all in order that our democracy—the social base of which is widening—becomes truly and fully a participative one.

CHANGES AND DIVERSITY

None of the identities, whether in the form of communities or in the form of segments, have ever remained frozen in time and space. One need not go far into history to see how identities have evolved. One has only to compare colonial ethnography and the PoI to identify the areas of change. There are five of them. First, the myths of origin differ sharply. As the movement towards political equality grows, the old myths of origin marked by the notion of degradation are discarded. The current perception of origin reflects a new sense of self-respect. Second, the old varna hierarchy seems to have collapsed or been gradually replaced by the three-tier structure of high, middle, and low positions. Third, there has been a range of occupational diversifications within a community, breaking the old nexus between a community and its traditional occupation. Fourth, there has been a pervasive impact of the development process. Finally, the mutual perceptions and relationships between communities, particularly modern relationships, are being radically altered with political and economic change.

It should also be noted that the relationships between the main communities and their segments have been a dynamic one. The old endogamous units or jatis within a community or caste have broken down, and the caste or the community has emerged as the larger endogamous unit. This is also one aspect of the consolidation of a community.

The extent of diversities existing in the country have alarmed some observers, even serious scholars, who believe that identifying—much less, studying—such diversities will be an invitation to disaster, break up the country and society, and so on. Diversities cannot be ignored but should be observed to see how they function. They are natural, native, part of our biological, linguistic, and cultural heritage, and without diversities we would not have survived as a civilization, or as a cultural system. Diversities are intrinsic not only to human evolution but also to human existence. They form a pattern of their own; they have a rhythm of their own.

And yet, various cultural and linguistic traits tend to coalesce in their own formations, in a manner which is natural, spontaneous, and effortless. Diversities, linkages, variation of traits and their convergence—they always go together—are the components of our biological, linguistic, and cultural heritage.

So much of diversity and so many of the linkages are located within the civilizational framework that the people of India have built up over the centuries. Both are reflected at the cognitive levels, in different schools of philosophies. There has not only been an understanding of self amidst diversity, but also a wiling acceptance of the other. Out of the objective reality of diversities has emerged an understanding of them, which, in spite of conflict and tension and occasional bloodbath, has generally endured. Out of this understanding has emerged a spirit of tolerance also. These diversities have flourished in a state of relative cultural freedom. Therefore, they go with freedom. Diversities and linkages, freedom and tolerance go together.

EFFECTS OF ECONOMIC GLOBALIZATION

A question that arises is whether the cultural diversities will survive or fade away with the globalization of the economy. A high priest of economic globalization recently observed in Delhi that while the economy is being globalized, governance remains national, and culture continues to be local and ethnic. There are fears not only in the developing countries about Western hegemonization of indigenous cultures, but also in some sections of the people in the developed counties about the possible impact of economic globalization on cultural homogenization. The question, therefore, that is being asked everywhere is whether culture, like economy, will also become globalized or homogenized. The answer to this question lies in the understanding of culture. If we take a long-term view of culture and see it as a river that absorbs many streams and flows on, then we shall be able to take a balanced view of the changes that are likely to occur. There is no doubt that some aspects of culture like food habit, dress, music, and so on, which are even ordinarily more prone to change, will be influenced, particularly for those who join the international circuit or those who are directly exposed to global influences. Such changes have occurred throughout history but the pace of change is much faster, almost mind-boggling, today. There are many other aspects of culture that might not experience the same impact of change, or might not change at all, for people in various age groups. In fact, there is a possibility that with the perceived threat to identity, a return to the roots might be faster as one can see in the movements of the indigenous peoples or in the environmental movements all across the world.

As we observed in the beginning, we have been able to generate, under the PoI, a composite profile of the people of India in its biological, cultural, and linguistic dimensions. However, the process of updating the material and generating fresh material and perspectives on change has to continue. The database has to be continually updated and enlarged to meet the requirements of the people. The Department of Biotechnology (in the Ministry of Science and Technology) has identified a number of projects on genomic diversities. On the basis of the cultural data generated by the PoI project, efforts are now being made to explore the molecular basis of genetic variation among some of our population groups. As we have covered only 800 communities under various parameters of anthropometrics and genetic surveys under the PoI, it should be possible now to launch a pan-Indian survey of all populations, with the new tools of molecular biology. A second phase of the PoI cultural project is also on, to analyse the traits at a natural level and in greater depth. The possibilities of a linguistic survey are being discussed, though mutedly. Language does not always divide but can serve as an instrument of integration. Language is a microcosm of many influences, which are absorbed as it grows and spreads. Therefore, we may look forward to the emergence of a more composite profile of all communities of India, in the first or second decade of the next century.

9

Pluralism, Synthesis, Unity in Diversities, Diversities in Unity[*]

PLURALISM

This chapter discusses pluralism at the cognitive level. First, we take up Anekantavada as a theory of diversity, probably the first of its kind, and as a tool of investigation and of understanding society. Anekantavada has its critics but almost everybody accepts that it is empirical, dynamic, realist, and pluralist.

It should be noted that while diversity of perceptions, approaches, and practices are recognized by some schools including those of the idealist philosophy, it is Anekantavada described by S. Radhakrishnan as a doctrine of realistic pluralism that tries to explore diversity logically and in depth (Radhakrishnan, 2004).

We are told that there are three tenets of Anekantavada. One, that there is a possibility of many perceptions of an object; two that everything is relative and multi-dimensional; and three, that there is

[*] Based on a talk on Anekanta given in May 2002 as part of the Anekanta series at the India International Centre under the auspices of the Jain Vishwa Bharti Institute.

an inbuilt co-existence of opposites, that one dimension is as possible as another and it is only in relation to other factors like time, place, and context that one dimension gains predominance over another. All this is subsumed under the doctrine of *syadavada* or *saptabhangi*. From the acceptance of the multi-dimensional nature of objects and their probability is derived the moral imperative of *ahimsa* or non-violence.

We thus see in Anekantavada a recognition of diversity, relativity, dynamism, and change which is of profound importance in under-standing society. Society too is multi-dimensional, consisting of multiple and contradictory trends, and variations in all their aspects which are bewildering in their range and depth. Some processes acquire salience owing to a combination of factors. Then they dissolve and another formation emerges. It is almost like a dialectical process, which goes on all the time, at all places, and in all communities. The world is in a flux; it is chaotic, uncertain, unpredictable. The social sciences have moved from unary to binary to multinary perceptions.

Variation has been described as an attribute of all living beings, or *jivas*—a philosophical principle which goes against the trends towards homogenization or hegemonization.

Over the past twenty years, we have been exploring diversity and affinities among Indian populations. A few findings may be discussed here. First, South Asia is now regarded as the most hybridized region of the world where various genepools intermingled. Second, the Indian subcontinent, next only to Brazil and Indonesia, is ecologically the most diverse and the richest repository of plant genes. Third, India has the largest number of languages (321) and scripts (25). Fourth, India has the largest number of ethnic groups—about 3,000 core groups, 10,000 endogamous groups, and 80,000 components of groups such as synonyms, segments, titles, and surnames. Lastly, nowhere else in the world has there been such a convergence of all types of diversity as in India.

Diversity is one aspect of the Indian formation. Through all forms of interactions, conflicts, and struggles there have emerged affinities in all domains. We are mostly a mixed people, and there is no genetical basis to either caste or varna. The human genom sequencing achieved recently suggests that we are all kin under the skin and yet there are variations. No two human beings are absolutely similar. There are more variations in terms of morphological and genetical traits within a community than between communities. Our languages belong to five different language families that have interacted and borrowed vocabulary and syntax. Bilingualism is high. The communities have interacted in space and time, and developed a culture of interaction or a composite culture which shows the extent of sharing, togetherness, and rootedness (of most of them). It has happened naturally and spontaneously as part of a civilizational process, at the level of the people.

Diversities and affinities are best seen at the regional or micro level. Each major region of India, and some of its sub-regions, are mini Indias, meeting grounds for various streams with their own cluster of communities with their titles, surnames, synonyms and segments, their languages and dialects, folk culture, and folk religion. Everyone of us is a microcosm.

However, we should not romanticize either diversity or affinity in general terms. Both are accommodated within an order of hierarchies which are unequal and iniquitous. We have a very unequal society, which becomes sometimes a violent one, in which all types of atrocities are committed against all—women, children, Dalit, tribes, and others.

Within this broad context of our studies in diversity and affinity, we should share some information about the Jains. But first about Lord Mahavira who demonstrated austerity of the most extreme kind—the nakedness of the spirit. Jainism gave the world the most revolutionary message of non-violence, and preached and practised it in an absolute sense, both at normative and behavioural levels. We are always puzzled as as to why the Buddha and Mahavira never met even though they shared the same annual circuit from Vaishali to Rajgir (because their paths never crossed and they represented two different paradigms, one of extreme austerity and the other of the middle path), why a religion that preached non-violence produced a Kharavela and generals in the army of the Rashtrakutas and the Chalukyas, and why a religion that preached non-stealing (*asteya*) and non-hoarding (*aparagriha*) should produce traders and businessmen. Probably the answer lies in the theory of Anekantavada which speaks of the co-existence of opposites, or the fact that the principles of non-stealing and non-hoarding shaped a lifestyle of simplicity and thrift, *a la* Max Weber, that made for accumulation, or more seriously in the working of historical processes, and the fact that life and culture have always been creative, resilient, ongoing, and have always reached out to new challenges, lying beyond the limits of religion.

We have studied 100 Jain communities all across India, noted the enormous scale of occupational diversification beyond the stereotypes of trade and business that has occurred, the range of progress and advancement that this small community has registered, and the enormous contributions that it has been making to the development of language, literature, culture, and economy through the ages, and to the understanding of Indian pluralism. Through history the Jains have moved from eastern to western India, where they are present in sizeable numbers as far as their communities are concerned. In spite of a homogenous religion with two sects, Jain society is marked by division and hierarchy, differentiation and stratification, rootedness in local culture, language, and kinship structure. Jain society is in transition. Sex ratio is adverse and therefore women related issues need to be addressed as well.

There does not seem to be any direct or organic linkage between diversity of the kind we have discussed earlier at the objective level, and diversity as perceived at the cognitive level. It is interesting to see how the classical texts including lexicographical works identify, list up, and sometimes describe, ecological features such as hills, valleys, rivers, oceans, deserts, pastures, and forests, and finally the peoples— from the Mahabharata, which is the first ethnographic work and the first lexicon of Jambudvipa, to Amarkosh, *Ain-i-Akbari* and *Varna Ratnakar* and through many similar works undertaken at the regional level. In Tamil Nadu there are Jain lexicons from the tenth century onwards and elsewhere we have an impressive literature on diversity. In fact, this pre-colonial heritage needs to be explored further to see how diversity was perceived, identified, and documented in various ways. The Indian mind was preoccupied with diversity, dissection, categorization, and classification.

SYNTHESIS

The colonial scholars held that India was never a nation, but only a geographical expression. To this the nationalists pointed out that it had always been a cultural unity. The lexicographical works that inventorized mountains, rivers, peoples among others conveyed a sense of connectivity and territorial integrity.

The nationalists spoke of synthesis and assimilation as the hallmark of Indian culture. Sri Aurobindo wrote:

India's national life will then be founded on her natural strengths and the principle of unity in diversity which has always been normal to her and its fulfillment the fundamental course of her being and its very nature, the Many in the One, would place her on the sure foundation of her Swabhava and Swadharma. (Sen, 2003)

The idea of unity in diversity emerged in the writings of some of the British ethnographers and historians. As H.H. Risley says:

Beneath the manifold diversity of physical and social type, language, custom and religion which strikes the observer in India, there can still be discerned, as Mr. Yusuf Ali has pointed out, a certain 'underlying uniformity of life from the Himalayas to Cape Camorin. There is in fact an Indian character, a general Indian personality, which we cannot resolve into its component elements. (Risley, 1915)

From uniformity to unity was the second step. The historian Vincent Smith spoke categorically of unity in diversity:

India offers unity in diversity. The underlined unity being less obvious than the superficial diversity and its nature and limitations merit exposition. The mere fact that the name India conveniently designates a subcontinental idea does not help to unify history and more than the existence of the name Asia could make the history of that Continent feasible. Though the unity sought must be of the nature more fundamental than that implied in the currency of a geographical term. (cited in Indira Gandhi Memorial Trust, 2003: 28)

The nationalists took up the theme of unity in diversity. However, Partition was a traumatic experience. Unity in diversity was a mantra chanted ritually on every occasion. President Neelam Sanjiva Reddy was probably the first president to speak of a plural society in 1976. In the 1980s, there was a new confidence in our diversity. Diversity came alive on Doordarshan, in the media, and through various festivals; festivals of India and Apna Utsav were the most important cultural events of the period.

Since the 1960s there has been an explosion of information about diversity. An enormous amount of knowledge became available about ethnic communities, their movements, and pluralism. Movements for self-determination occurred all across the world. Movements for conservation of environment, human rights, rights of Indigenous people, and so on, focused on diversity and identity. Therefore there was at the academic level, a leap from the notion of unity in diversity to the notion of diversity in unity, underlining the growing knowledge of diversity. Prime Minister Vajpayee in his Red Fort speech of 2003 spoke both of unity in diversity and diversity in unity.

The ethical implications of the theory of diversity first propounded by Anekantavada and debated now at various fora should be considered carefully. Diversity recognizes identity, uniqueness of all traits and cultures and their autonomy, and communities' freedom and role in self management of resources. Therefore tolerance based on understanding, which is the essence of non-violence as propounded by Anekantavada, and as accepted all over now, is the tool that humankind will need to fight the forces unleashed by fundamentalism in the present century.

10

Diversity, Heterogeneity, and Integration

An Ideological Perspective*

This chapter attempts the delineation of the existing ethnographic scenario covering ecological, genetic, linguistic, and cultural aspects, and the heterogeneity of groups, particularly religious groups. Then it discusses the rootedness of groups in various eco-cultural niches, and the processes of interdependence in day-to-day life, leading to a large measure of integration of groups. Against the background of this ethnographic configuration, the chapter discusses the ideological question, syncretism, composite culture, the freedom struggle, and the post-colonial perspectives on diversity, autonomy, and integration.

I

As discussed elsewhere, few regions in the world have such a range of diversity as the Indian subcontinent, particularly India as it is

* The data on diversity and heterogeneity of religious formations is mainly derived from the People of India project. See K.S. Singh, 1992, *People of India: An Introduction*, Calcutta: Anthropological Survey of India, and K.S. Singh (ed.), 1996–8, *People of India: India's Communities*, New Delhi: Anthropological Survey of India.

constituted today. There is an extraordinary range of diversity in terms of biological, linguistic, and cultural traits among the people of India. Genetically, most Indians are a highly mixed people. The morphological and genetic variation among populations, it is stated, occurs more within a community than between communities. There are as many as 325 community-specific languages and dialects belonging to five language families, and twenty-five scripts are in use. There are as many as 2,795 communities and about 80,000 segments, synonyms, titles, and surnames.

The Constitution of India categorizes most of the people in terms of the Scheduled Tribes, the Scheduled Castes, the Other Backward Classes, and the religious and linguistic minorities. Cutting across these categories are also religious and occupational groups, situated in rural and urban locations. At one level, the communities are projected as homogeneous, as they also perceive themselves as sharing many a common trait. But such groups are also heterogeneous, located in various regions and rooted in local kinship systems, social practices, languages and dialect, and so on. These communities including castes, tribes, etc., see themselves now as political communities, engaged in the struggle for a share in the regional and national power structures.

The religious communities at one level consider themselves homogeneous as they follow tenets of their religion which also lays down the social norms to be followed. Religious identities are being consolidated, as they distance themselves from one another and withdraw themselves from the shared cultural space. Even a pluralistic religion such as Hinduism is being 'sanitized'. At the same time, in the spirit of attempts at homogenization, religious conglomerations continue to remain heterogeneous (K.S. Singh, 1992; K.S. Singh [ed.], 1998b; Thapar, 1996).

We may now discuss the structure, composition, and distribution of major religious groups. Hindu communities, 3,539 in all, are spread all over the country except in Lakshadweep. Hindu society, which articulates diversities of continental dimensions, is marked by division, hierarchy, and linkages. The Hindu communities show an extraordinary range of heterogeneity—genetic, morphological (being of a mixed group), linguistic, and cultural. Social divisions widely exist in the form of phratries, moieties, clans, sub-castes, and sub-tribes. Hierarchy with divisions exists among a quarter of the communities. In Hindu society 21.6 per cent communities place themselves at the high level, 46.7 per cent at the middle level, and 31.1 per cent at the low level. The notion of varna is integral to Hinduism, with as many as 80 per cent of Hindu communities aware of the varna order and a larger number (61.9 per cent) recognizing their place—as a Brahmana (10 per cent), as a Kshatriya (20 per cent), as a Vaishya (10.8 per cent), and as a Sudra (36.9 per cent). Rootedness in local cultures explains the variation in marriage practices, including cross-cousin MBD (16.2 per cent), FSD (39.6 per cent), and uncle-niece (23.7 per cent) marriages; sororate (junior) is practised by a larger number of communities (47.6 per cent), and sororate (senior) among a smaller number (4.2 per cent). Junior levirate preponderates. Adult marriage is now practised among almost all communities, but child marriage is also reported (4.7 per cent). Monogamy is the rule (99.4 per cent), but there also exists polygyny, sororal (13.4 per cent) and non-sororal (21.8 per cent) alliances, polyandry, and fraternal (0.3 per cent) and non-fraternal (0.1 per cent) relationships. All types of families co-exist on a larger scale among the Hindus—the nuclear family (89 per cent), vertically extended family (48.8 per cent), and horizontally extended family (11.2 per cent). Male equigeniture is the rule among the majority of the communities (85 per cent). There is also the matrilineal system, with elements of female ultimo geniture (0.2 per cent) and female equigeniture (0.5 per cent). Succession generally goes to the eldest son (96.4 per cent); in a smaller number of cases (0.3 per cent) the eldest daughter inherits, as does the youngest son (0.5 per cent), or youngest daughter (0.1 per cent), or nephew (1.1 per cent). Restrictions on exchange of water and food have been extensively relaxed, but they have not disappeared entirely from villages. At one level, the Hindus are consolidating themselves as a religious community with a larger measure of sharing, promoted by reformists and activists and facilitated by education and communication.

The Muslim communities (584) are distributed over almost all the states, in the following order: Uttar Pradesh (70), Jammu and Kashmir (59), Gujarat (87), Rajasthan (44), Andhra Pradesh (38), Bihar (41),

Karnataka (27), Delhi (30), Maharashtra (25), Tamil Nadu (23), Madhya Pradesh (26), West Bengal (21), Himachal Pradesh (19), Kerala (10), and Puducherry (10); in Lakshadweep, Assam, Haryana, and Chandigarh (7 each); in Andaman and Nicobar Islands, Tripura, and Daman and Diu (3 each); in Nagaland and Orissa (2 each); and in Manipur, Sikkim, Goa, Dadar and Nagar Haveli (1 each). Even though the Muslims uniformly share the tenets of their faith, they are rooted in various ecological riches and cultural systems. The Muslim communities are also thus heterogeneous and differ from one another in biological, linguistic, and cultural traits. The Muslims are mainly situated in rural–urban (103) settings. Even Muslim communities such as the Watal, Lalbegi, Madari/Kalander claim the status of the Scheduled Castes, and nineteen communities have been returned as Scheduled Tribes. Of the total number of Muslim communities, a very large number, 60.8 per cent, has migrated to their present habitat in recent years. While Urdu has been returned as the mother tongue by a majority of Muslims, 46.27 per cent of them have also returned the scheduled/regional languages as their mother tongues. Social divisions among Muslims exist on a relatively smaller scale in the form of clans (22.4 per cent), sects (9.4 per cent), sub-castes (10.6 per cent), bands, and sub-tribes. Hierarchy with social division also exists. Differentiation is reported at social, economic, religious (sects), occupational, and territorial levels. Egalitarianism in the domain of religion is a well-known feature of Muslim society. However, stratification exists: a relatively small segment of Muslim communities (15.6 per cent) perceive themselves as occupying high positions; most of them (58.6 per cent) see themselves at the middle level; and a smaller percentage at the low level (28.5 per cent). While the norm of community endogamy operates among most of the Muslim communities, there are various levels of exogamy, such as clan exogamy (9.6 per cent), and even gotra exogamy (6.7 per cent), village exogamy (7.2 per cent), and surname exogamy (3.9 per cent). Hypergamy is reported on a smaller scale (3.6 per cent), and even hypogamy (1.2 per cent). It is obvious that some of the Muslim communities are rooted in the local kinship system. The same is true of marriages. While parallel cousin marriages, both FSD and MBD, are widely practised (68.7 per cent and 65.8 per cent respectively) as per the Shariat, there are Muslim communities who prefer cross cousins' parallel cousin marriages. The Assamese Muslims avoid both cross cousin and parallel cousin marriage, while the Meos, Tadvis, and Nahals avoid parallel cousin marriages. Clan exogamy is reported by Rajput Muslims and some other converted higher groups (Siddiqui, 1993). The incidence of cross cousin FSD is higher (81.2 per cent), as is cross cousin MBD (2.5 per cent), particularly in the southern states. Interestingly, both junior sororate (50.5 per cent) and senior sororate (7.4 per cent) are practised. Junior levirate also prevails (37 per cent), and, on a smaller scale, with *gauna* (2.7 per cent). Marriage by negotiation is the common mode of acquiring mates among the majority of the communities (97.9 per cent). The other modes of acquiring mates practised by them include exchange (20.2 per cent), mutual consent (18.7 per cent), elopement (2.2 per cent), service (1.7 per cent), purchase (0.9 per cent)—mostly among the 'tribalized groups'—and so on.

The marriage symbols shared by Muslims with non-Muslims include wearing bangles (26.2 per cent), nose stud/pin (19.5 per cent), toering (14.6 per cent), *tali/mangalsutra* (11.5 per cent), vermillion (9.1 per cent), finger ring (8.6 per cent), ear ring (6.8 per cent), nose ring (10.6 per cent), and *bindi* (4.8 per cent). Occupationally, the Muslims are more heterogeneous than any other religious community. While land is the economic resource for many, a majority of them are landless (48.5 per cent). A smaller number depends on fishing (5.5 per cent) and on forest resources (6.3 per cent). A majority of Muslim communities are self-employed (49.1 per cent), engaged in occupations such as business (52.4 per cent) or in private service (45 per cent). Various other occupations in which they are engaged include horticulture (2.9 per cent), sericulture (0.9 per cent), industry (9.1 per cent), industrial work (16.3 per cent), textile weaving (5.3 per cent), textile dyeing (2.1 per cent), masonry (6.8 per cent), woodwork (4.5 per cent), skin and hidework (2.1 per cent), specialized service (5 per cent), skilled (14.6 per cent) and non-skilled labour (20.4 per cent), and so on. A professional middle class is emerging among the Muslims which is playing a critical role in building up modern inter-community linkages. This consists of entrepreneurs/businessmen (62.7 per cent), scholars including students (26.2 per cent), white-collar employees (52.9 per cent), teachers (52.2 per cent), administrators (28.9 per cent), engineers/doctors (34.6 per cent), village *panchayat* leaders (30.1 per cent), regional leaders (22.3 per cent), and so on.

The Christian communities are also heterogeneous like the other communities, as they are drawn from various socio-religious backgrounds, and from various categories of groups such as the Scheduled Castes and Scheduled Tribes and 'other' communities in various regions. Generally, a great many pre-conversion practices survive among the Christians who share a good deal with non-Christian communities. The Christian communities (339) are distributed mainly in the southern states such as Tamil Nadu (65), Andhra Pradesh (29), Karnataka (22), and Kerala (13), and in the north-eastern states such as Assam, Arunachal Pradesh (23), Manipur (23), Nagaland (19), Mizoram (15), Meghalaya (15), and Tripura (12). They also live in West Bengal (10), Maharashtra (14), Andaman and Nicobar Islands (9), Orissa (7), Goa (6), Bihar and Madhya Pradesh (5 each), and so on. Social divisions survive among most of them (76.1 per cent), such as phartries (15), moieties (9), clans (190; 56 per cent), and lineages (106; 31.3 per cent). There are sub-castes (9) and sub-tribes (23) among these communities. Hierarchy with social divisions exists among a large number. Most of the Christian communities are endogamous (95.3 per cent). Various levels of exogamy operate—clan exogamy (165; 48.7 per cent), even gotra exogamy (19; 5.6 per cent), surname exogamy (58; 17.1 per cent), and village exogamy (29; 8.6 per cent). Monogamy is the norm; however sororal polygyny (15 per cent) and non sororal polygyny (23.3 per cent) are also practised. Among marriage symbols,the tali/mangalsutra is widely worn among a large number of communities (45.4 per cent) followed by the more popular finger ring (30.4 per cent), vermillion (82; 24.2 per cent), and toe ring (79; 23.3 per cent). There is now a wide range of occupational diversification. Some of the traditional occupations have relatively declined. Many Christian communities, mostly tribals, were engaged in hunting and gathering (29.8 per cent), which has partly declined (18 per cent); similarly, fishing has declined to 86 per cent today from among the 101 communities involved earlier. The communities engaged in trapping of birds and animals (43) have mostly abandoned this occupation; only sixteen communities are now engaged in it. On the other hand, communities traditionally engaged in horticulture (27) have increased (to 49). Similarly, more Christian communities are now engaged in occupations such as liquor manufacture (4.7 per cent), shifting cultivation (25.1 per cent), terrace cultivation (13.9 per cent), settled cultivation (55.8 per cent), and animal husbandry (32.4 per cent). A good number of communities are also engaged in various other occupations such as business (51.9 per cent), trade (24.5 per cent), industry (10.9 per cent), government service (81.7 per cent), private service (58.7 per cent), textile spinning (4.4 per cent), and textile weaving (19.5 per cent). A small number of them are engaged in masonry, pottery, woodwork, salt making, skin- and hidework, ivory, bone- and horn-work, metalwork, etc., ranging from 1 to 5 per cent. A good number of Christian communities have returned to basket making (20.9 per cent), mat weaving (8.6 per cent), specialized service (5.9 per cent), skilled labour (189 per cent), and non-skilled labour (35.1 per cent) as their occupations. More Christian communities are engaged in the above occupations compared to the percentage of all other religious communities. The Christian communities have reported a much higher proportion of inter-community linkage and exchange, including inter-community marriage (52). A progressive religious community, they favour education of boys (88.2 per cent) but a relatively large number of communities favour education of girls (78 per cent) as well. Though boys are favoured for higher education, a relatively large number of communities prefer a high level of education for girls as well.

There are 130 Sikh communities living in Punjab (39), Delhi (20), Chandigarh (15), Haryana (17), Jammu and Kahsmir (5), Uttar Pradesh (5), Himachal Pradesh (8), Rajasthan (4), Andhra Pradesh (3), Maharashtra (3), Assam (2), West Bengal (2), and so on. In spite of the stress on egalitarianism in Sikhism the caste system exists, and social divisions are reported (90 per cent) in the form of clans (76.9 per cent), sects (12.3 per cent), and sub-castes (22.3 per cent). Hierarchy with social divisions is returned (26.9 per cent against 22.6 per cent). Differentiation is reported at social, economic, occupational, and territorial levels. There is a perception of the three-tier hierarchy. Fifty-three (40.8 per cent) communities perceive themselves as placed high, 45.4 per cent at the middle level, and 13.8 per cent are placed low. A majority of Sikh communities have land as their economic resource, but a very large number are landless. They are engaged in settled cultivation (31 per cent), in about (37.7 per cent), animal husbandry, industry, trade and business, government service, private service, and self employment, which is as high as 64.6 per cent as against the national average of 52 per cent. They are reported in small numbers in other occupations such as fishing, textile weaving, masonry, woodwork, skin- and hidework, basket making, skilled labour, and non-skilled labour.

The Buddhist communities (93), which constitute 2 per cent of all communities, are mainly distributed in Arunachal Pradesh (18), Assam (11), Uttar Pradesh (9), West Bengal (7), Himachal Pradesh (6), Jammu and Kashmir (6), Delhi (4), Andhra Pradesh (3), and so on. Most of the Buddhist communities belong to the Scheduled Tribes and share tribal characteristics. The neo-Buddhists, another important segment of the Buddhist community, consist of such groups as the Mihras and Jatavs, who are imbued with Baba Saheb B.R. Ambedkar's ideology, stressing equality and self-respect, and have pushed forward in the arena of politics and development.

The Jain communities, 100 in all, are distributed mainly in the central and western states such as Madhya Pradesh (18), Maharashtra, Rajasthan and Gujarat (13 each), and sporadically in Punjab (2), Bihar (3), Uttar Pradesh (2), Himachal Pradesh (2), and even in the states of Nagaland, Meghalaya, Assam, Jammu and Kashmir, West Bengal, Andhra Pradesh, Puducherry, Daman and Diu, Haryana, and Chandigarh. They are mostly located in rural–urban situations (58), followed by exclusive settlements in urban areas (34). A small number of them (8) also live in rural areas. Almost all of them are pure vegetarian (95 per cent against the national average of 16.05 per cent). Social divisions exist among Jain communities in the form of clans (76), lineages (28), sects (16), and sub-castes (38). Hierarchy with social divisions is reported among twenty-eight communities.

Differentiation operates at social (53), sectarian (26), occupational (14) levels, and so on. Most Jain communities (70 per cent) perceive themselves as placed at high and only a few at middle levels. The Jains share the kinship structure of the areas they are located in. Community endogamy is the norm. In the north and the west, the Jains practise cross cousin marriages, FSD (14 per cent) and MBD (15), and uncle–niece marriages (6). Sororate junior is allowed (44 per cent), and levirate junior is in vogue in a few communities (5 per cent). The Jains are mainly engaged in business (89 per cent), trade (63 per cent), and industry (30 per cent). Thirty-two communities depend on land as their economic resource. Nineteen communities are mainly landowning. Forty-one of them (41 per cent) are engaged in settled cultivation.

The Jains have now rapidly moved into government service (90 per cent), alongside private service (66 per cent), and self-employment (63 per cent). A few of them are in textile weaving (3), textile dyeing (2), woodwork, glass work, and jewellery making. While elsewhere the Jains are traders and businessmen, entrepreneurs and merchants, the Jains of Karnataka traditionally are mainly peasants and artisan groups (K.S. Singh, 1992; K.S. Singh [ed.], 1998b).

II

The preceding discussion on diversities and heterogeneity of religious groups, who generally project themselves as monolithic, sets the background for the discussion of the structures of interrelationship— and a few have been indicated above—and of interaction of work among all groups. This is best seen at the regional level in its eco-cultural linguistic dimensions. They are generally well adjusted within the regional system. It is here again that the rootedness of most of the communities, and the sharing of cultural and linguistic traits by them, is best explored. It is here again that various features of living together, in spite of occasional outbursts of tension and violence, are best seen in their enduring aspects. A few of these aspects may be briefly described:

(i) Most of the communities (as many as 83 per cent) are local, situated within the existing linguistic–cultural regions (K.S. Singh, 1992);

(ii) Many of the communities, including the Muslims, consider themselves as 'relatively' indigenous and regard others as later immigrants, as outsiders or *pardesis, mayangs, bangals,* and so on, even if they all belong to the same religious group (Siddiqui, 1993);

(iii) Most of the communities, irrespective of their religious labels, belong to the same or similar genepools, and share morphological and genetic traits (K.S. Singh, 1992; Siddiqui, 1993);

(iv) Most of the communities generally speak the same language/dialect within the region, and share folklores, rituals, putative kinships or ceremonial friendships, and so on (K.S. Singh, 1992);

(v) All share elements of hierarchy in the regional system, and forms of relationship, both vertical and horizontal (Siddiqui, 1993), even though there is a difference between inter-group relationships existing among Muslims and inter-caste relationships among Hindus;

(vi) The Muslims and their segments are appropriately ranked within the regional hierarchy of communities;

(vii) The economic interdependence of all communities of India is closely rooted in the resource endowment and resource utilization in each region of India. This interdependence may assume various forms of *jajmani* or patron–client relationship, cultivator–tenant relationship, artisan–customer relationship, and so on. This is the secular form of relationship cutting across religious divisions, and interlocking of different religious/sectarian strata in the regional context survives all riots and all attempts to disrupt them. No religious group is functionally exclusive, and all are closely intertwined in the struggle for subsistence, survival, and progress (K.S. Singh, 1992);

(viii) Participation in one another's religio-cultural activities is high, and in all, the incidence of sharing of traits is higher than expected (K.S. Singh, 1992).

Many communities of India, about 600 of them according to one estimate, are divided into religious segments. The Hindu–Sikh, Hindu–Jain, Hindu–Buddhist, and Hindu–Tribal share commensal and connubial relationships across religious divisions.

The Hindu–Muslim segments of the same lineage do not have connubial (in case of inter-marriage, they convert) or commensal relationships, but have other close links. In a cluster of villages called Sathe, that is, sixty villages lying within a hundred kilometre stretch in the Ghaziabad district of Uttar Pradesh, the Hindu and Muslim segments of the Chauhan lineage continue to share a unique relationship.

'Some of our brothers became Muslims while the others remained Hindu. All the same, we are from the same family. Our ancestors were one,' says Faiz Mukkadam.

The social lives of the two communities in the area are intertwined. When Ram Kali was asked to sing at the wedding in a Muslim family, she did not hesitate even for a moment as she started on *Bhaiya Regubir bhaat sware laiya* (Oh brother dear who is so like Lord Rama, bring beautiful presents when you come). Soon the strain was picked up by the women of the family. To them it did not matter that Rama was not their god. Ram Kali also relates how the Muslim women sang *Allah Allah kar ke to ye din aya, dulhan ne naya shringar rachaya* (It is by taking the name of Allah that this day has arrived and the bride has been adorned) during the wedding festivities of her daughter.

When a child is born, be it in a Muslim or a Hindu house, the words of the traditional song *Tere angana mein khelay Nandlala* (In your courtyard plays Lord Krishna) waft across the village along with the beat of the *dholak*. 'We sing the same songs; some of our ceremonies are also similar. Everyone in the village takes part in weddings and festivities in every home,' says Ram Kali ...

'Our style of living, dressing, weddings and other celebrations are almost the same. We hardly feel any difference. In fact, we also face the evil of dowry as the Hindu[s] do,' adds Sarvari, of a nearby village.

In the nearby hut, Kaneez is a trifle surprised when asked whether she invites Hindus to her family festivities. 'Of course, they are our relatives. We just take special care to cook separately for them because they are vegetarians. Those who are not, eat with us. We also take part in the festivities in their houses.'

Even the village temple is not out of bounds for the Muslims. Muslim children can be seen playing with their Hindu mates in the temple premises while worship goes on. Adjacent to the temple is the hut of a Muslim family.

'How can we forget that we are [of] the same blood? As long as we remember this and pass it on to our children, we will continue to live as brothers,' says Mehar Ali. (Saksena, 1994)

Scholars have generally noticed that the traditionally shared cultural space is shrinking and the secularized space is growing as more and more people interact in the secular sphere. The Muslims who were very much like Hindus in many parts of the country at the beginning of the colonial period, as stated in colonial ethnography, began to look less similar as religious identities were emphasized. Islamization and *tablighi* movements stressed separateness. And yet, as the People of India (PoI) project shows, in spite of sharpening of religious identities, the communities continue to share a great deal (see K.S. Singh, 1992), and their interaction in the secular sphere has survived growing stratification and Islamization (Bhatty, 1997), as have norms of clan exogamy and cross cousin marriages among many Muslim communities (Siddiqui, 1979, 1993). The Muslims follow the rules of gotra exogamy, adopt Hindu titles or surnames, sing the same songs at life-cycle ceremonies, share their style of living, dressing, and so on. There are Sathes in every corner of India.

The folklores of almost every part of India reflect a synthesis, an effortless, spontaneous intermingling of various steams. There are, no doubt, references to conflicts arising out of animosities, but towards the end of the story, all is well, all end in harmony. Folk minds cannot stand confrontation for long. In western Madhya Pradesh and Rajasthan, *pir*s blessed the founding of kingdoms by Hindu princes. Similarly, the oral epic of Devnarayan, recited by the pastoral and farming communities of the Gujjars, commemorates inter-caste conflict but also re-union. The Rajput chiefs and Gujjars became *dharam*-brothers, sharing kinship relationships and conflicts simultaneously (Aditya Malik, 1994). A similar strand of conflict and reunion runs through many oral traditions in different parts of the country.

The various sects in India have not only quarrelled among themselves but have also closely interacted. Many medieval sects preached egalitarianism, attacked the caste system, and advocated understanding and tolerance. In spite of the 'polemical character' of the preaching of some of the founders of the modern sects, they too were influenced by each other, and showed a measure of respect and understanding in day-to-day dealings. There was never a time when diversity of perceptions did not exist within a religious system, even as the theologians tried to grapple with the pluralistic situation. Among the various Islamic sects in northern India is the numerically preponderant Barelvi sect which is the least critical of the tradition of customary practices among Muslims, as against the Deobandhis who are moderate reformists and critical of traditional elements, and others who stand for purging Muslim society of all extra-Islamic customs (Siddiqui, 1993).

A contemporary movement known as Swadhyaya or 'Study of the Self', currently underway in 12,000 to 15,000 villages in twelve states of India, based on the philosophy and teachings of Panduranga Shastri Athwale or Dadaji, has addressed many aspects of social problems such as inequality, and advocated rural development with the exploitation and enlargement of indigenous resources for the benefit of all. For our purposes, it is interesting to note that it has brought together communities divided by religions and social inequality.

The village of Herala in the district Junagarh of Gujarat is completely *Swadhyayi*. It comprises forty households of Karodia Rajputs, seventy households of Harijans, and ten households of Siddi Muslims. Herala had had a long history of discrimination against Koli Harijans and Siddi Muslims. Says Mangal Bhai, leader of the Siddi Muslims:

We were being treated like animals, in fact a little worse. We had no rights, no dignity, no power and perhaps no life in human terms. With the coming of Swadhyaya, all this is a thing of the distant past. There is no discrimination of any kind now, no exploitation, no quarrels, no strife and no dissent. We are all one, all children of the same god. We Siddis regularly come to the *amritalay* (temple). We have helped to build it. Likewise, our mosque was built by Hindus. (Sinha, 1998)

That syncretism is not a medieval relic, and not dying, was brought home by Saeed Naqvi's serial, *Hamari Virasat*, telecast on Doordarshan. This serial meticulously collected and vividly demonstrated the known and the not-so-well-known living traditions of syncretism in which Hindus and Muslims interacted closely at many shrines. Spread far and wide, these shrines and the practices in vogue there still continue to bear testimony to the strength of syncretism. The various streams of Bhakti, Sufi, and Tantra blend in rural India. In western India, the blending of these streams reached its culmination in the Shirdi Sai Baba cult. In the Barak valley of Assam, the Shah Pir has a niche in every

Kalibari. The story goes that the Sufis came from Silchar, exorcised witchcraft which was and is still rampant, preached Islam in the local language, and showed tolerance and understanding towards mother goddess cults; on their part, the followers of these cults also showed an understanding and tolerance towards Sufism.

The ethnographic scenario of diversity and heterogeneity and the structure of interdependence, sharing, and linkages existing among people in various regions are now overlaid, even obscured, by an acrimonious ideological debate on the nature of the identities of our people, the relationship between communities, their status, and rights, being articulated in essentially religious idioms. All over the world fundamentalism is on the rise, in all religions. In this country, all religious communities who shared the common space and built up a shared heritage have now been emphasizing their separate identities, promoting their consolidation, distancing themselves from one another, and seeking to protect their rights and privileges. There is very little understanding now of how religions in this country have been known to have shared the ideas of all religions as being positive, equal, similar in their basics. This was emphasized in the course of the freedom struggle and the Indian Renaissance, but now appears to be a romantic dream. Similarly, cultures—larger than religion—are being focused on as distinct from one another. The very notion of composite culture is being questioned (Madan, 1998).

The concept of shared cultural traditions, of linkages that brought us together and that still brings us together in day-to-day life in our struggle for survival, is ignored. In fact, culture is no longer seen in its entirety, as it unfolds in everyday life or as it has existed through history. It was not a medieval phenomenon only. It could be traced to the very early times (Shrimali, 1998). It covered all aspects of life, in rural and urban; it permeated all strata of populations (Momin, 1998).

At the heart of all communal debates in India is the medieval factor. All discussions boil down to Hindu–Muslim relations. The medieval factor in Indian history has often been explored to define the current level of relations among religious communities. There is little doubt that there was considerable violence and bigotry in the early phase of encounter of different religions or cultures or civilizations in the ancient and medieval periods. Hindus and Jains, Shaivites and Vaishnavites widely differed and often acted violently against each other and each other's institutions. Abul Fazl recounts the facets of sectarian conflict in the medieval period, and laments that the first encounter of sects was often bitter and violent. Alberuni's first reaction to the Hindus was far from temperate. But as the conquerors and those who came with them settled down, a process of interaction with those who were there from the earlier period began in all spheres of administration, politics, languages, literature, and art, and the medieval phenomenon of composite culture emerged. But by all accounts, bigotry and violence in India were on a relatively smaller scale than elsewhere, partly because a ruler tried to understand the pluralistic situation his regime was situated in, and partly because there was the need to maintain a measure of harmony and social stability that was necessary for the exercise of political power (see Z.U. Malik, 1990). The medieval period was instrumental in the further development of the Indian civilization, particularly in matters of ideas, culture, and technology, and efforts at spiritual synthesis (see Ali, 1990). One interesting aspect was the rise of vernacular languages, bhasas, and of regional identities as defined by them within which were located groups of people known by jati, like *kaum, kabila,* and so on. Abul Fazl mentions the dominant lineages of zamindars in various regions of Akbar's empire, which are strikingly similar to the dominant sections among the jatis and communities today. The second aspect was the understanding, gradually growing, among the followers of Islam and Hinduism, of respective religious tenets, and a tolerant attitude towards the religious susceptibilities of one another. The inscriptions of the distant 'tribal' Chero and Gond rulers open with a simultaneous invocation to both Rama and Allah. Rama Kumbha, who defeated Sultan Bahadur Shah of Gujarat, raided the Victory Tower which has the name Allah inscribed on the walls of one of its storeys (Ali, 1990). This mindset obviously acknowledged the existence of two religious streams, their equality, without giving up one's own identity. When the medieval period came to a close, it bequeathed upon the next age this understanding of the pluralities at the religious level, and what is more important, a respect for each other's sensibilities. The princely states—and smaller *thikana*s and later the traditional zamindars of the colonial period—inherited from the Mughal rule some of the symbols of social harmony such as celebration of festivals and festivities, endowments in each other's religious centres, and other such traditions. The Gandhian movement and later the Bhoodan movement led by Acharya Vinoba Bhave emphasized common celebration of all religious festivals. A fresh understanding of the nature of the symbiosis between Islam and Hinduism is being attempted today.

The notion of composite culture was invoked by the nationalists in the course of the freedom struggle, and it received a boost through the writings, among others, of Mahatma Gandhi, Jawaharlal Nehru, and Maulana Abul Kalam. The historian S. Gopal tells us how Nehru approached this theme in his *The Discovery of India*:

The unity of India was an emotional reality rooted in history rather than mere geographical creation or an imposed standardization of externals. Beneath the shared intellectual and cultural life among the educated was a common popular culture of philosophy, history, myth and legend. Existing traditions were respected, adapted and changed to meet new circumstances and ways of thought and at the same time new traditions were developed. Every challenge of incursion of foreign elements was dealt with successfully by absorption and a new synthesis. Islam had come to India as a religion. Centuries before it came as a political force, it had been received with the usual tolerance. When later, the rulers happened to be Muslim, the essential unity of Indian life was not vitally affected and the new rulers rarely interfered with the ways and customs of the people. A composite culture developed in such fields as architecture, food, dress and music. Even the two religions, Hinduism and Islam, influenced each other. (Gopal, 1986)

According to C.A. Bayly, till about the middle of the eighteenth century, it was a 'predominantly syncretic culture', with no sense of social separateness (Bayly quoted by Gopal, 1986: 208). 'Communalism as a distant phenomenon emerged only about the middle of the nineteenth century' (Gopal, 1986) as religious disputes mixed with economic antagonism and political ambitions. The partition of the country, the riots, and migration of populations seemed to have had temporarily dealt a death blow to the notion of composite culture that was the bedrock of Indian nationalism.

However, the nationalists were also aware of the existence of religious, ethnic, and regional identities (kaum), and of their relationships. As Maulana Azad said to the Indian Muslims migrating to Pakistan, in 1947:

You are leaving your motherland. Do you know what the consequences will be? Your frequent exoduses, such as this, will weaken the Muslims of India. A time may come when the various Pakistani regions start asserting their separate identities. Bengali, Punjabi, Sindhi, Baloch may declare themselves separate *qaims*. Will your position in Pakistan at that time be anything better than uninvited guests? The Hindu can be your religious opponent, but not your regional and national opponent. You can deal with this situation. But in Pakistan, at any time you may have to face regional and national opposition; before this kind of opposition you will be helpless. (Khushwant Singh, 1998)

Orientalism generated an enormous amount of interest in the ethnography of India. The colonial period with its ethnographic information and the census data created taxonomic groups such as the tribes and exterior or depressed castes. The identities as Hindus, Muslims, and Sikhs were sharply focused on from the middle of the nineteenth century. Each group was generally represented as homogeneous and projected as a separate political community vying for a share in the political power. The colonial administration patronized these groups and supported their attempts at homogenization in terms of the textual prescriptions and their elite's perceptions. One result of such consolidation of 'orthodox' groups and 'orthodox' norms was that the fluidity of the social situation that marked the pre-colonial period was ignored, and the diversities that characterized eco-social formulations in India were swept aside. Various communities of India had graduated to a strange mutual understanding in the eighteenth century; the symbols of communal harmony adopted by the Mughal court had percolated to the regional centres of power. The Hindus and Muslims had come to recognize and respect each other's religion even though there were generally no commensal and connubial relationships between them. All this changed in the colonial period, with the portrayal of these groups as autonomous, almost divested of commonalities of a composite culture that was evolving.

The process of religious consolidation has proceeded apace in the post-colonial period. The international scenario is marked by the rise of religious fundamentalism and ethnic identities, and similar developments within the nation-state have continued with distancing of religious identities from one another, and blurring of the vision of composite culture. There are, no doubt, also countervailing processes at work. The movement for conservation of the environment, the struggle of the indigenous people, human rights issues cutting cross national boundaries, have focused on ecological–cultural diversities, heterogeneity, and identities. Historical and ethnographical studies undertaken in recent years have also highlighted linkages between groups, their close interaction, and their common roots. Therefore, first, the ideological perspective today should take into account diversities, heterogeneity of groups, the patterns of interaction, sharing and linkages, that exist spontaneously, naturally, and necessarily among various sections of people at all levels, in their day-to-day life. Second, the nation, which grew out of the anti-colonial struggle, should embrace all identities, big and small, and should unequivocally stand for recognition of the equal rights of all groups that make up the nation. Understanding, tolerance, and respect for each other's identity should be the nationalist credo today as it was during the freedom struggle, and as it should be in the struggle to create the human and humane order.

The ideological currents and their impact apart, the collective life at the grassroots level proceeds at its own rhythm and momentum. The interdependence of communities engaged in the struggle for existence continues, even in time of stress. The logic, the compulsion of living together in the local situation, further explains the process of sharing and the structure of linkages existing among communities. The political analysts may see in occasional flare-ups an end to this idyllic ethnographic scenario, but ethnic traits survive catastrophes. The noted litterateur, K.S. Duggal, during a recent visit to Pakistan to attend the wedding of a friend's son, was 'heartened' to hear the Muslim women sing:

Why do you stand under the Chandran tree, daughter?
I wait for my father to tell him
It's time to look for a match.
What type of a match would you like, my daughter?
One like the moon in the stars,
And Krishna Kanhaiya among the gods.

(Duggal, 1997)

The nation-state of such diversities as ours, with a rich composite culture, should continue to re-emphasize and recreate symbols that hold us together, and should continue to explore areas of cooperation, understanding, and tolerance among various sections of our people who, too, must understand and affirm pluralism. There is no alternative to living together.

11

Our Composite Culture and Society, Our Linkages

I

Any discussion of composite culture and society has to be located within the framework of information and knowledge about diversities. Firstly, South and South-east Asia, particularly the Indian subcontinent, is now described as the most hybridized region in the world where various genetical streams met, making it a genetical laboratory. The intermingling of gene pools inspired Rabindranath Tagore's composition 'Bharat Tirtha' (1912). In spite of the occasional revival of the theory of race to serve a separatist agenda, the idea that there is no genetical basis for caste and varna, which are essentially cultural constructs, has prevailed. Secondly, the subcontinent has been among the most ecologically diverse regions in the world, and India next only to Indonesia and Brazil is the richest in ecological resources. Thirdly, India has been linguistically the most heterogeneous region in the world as well, with 321 community-specific languages and twenty-five functioning scripts. Fourthly, there is also the most extraordinary range of ethnic diversity with 3,000 communities, 10,000 endogamous groups or anthropologically defined communities—which is the delight and despair of geneticists engaged in human genome projects—and 80,000 components including synonyms, segments, titles, ard sur-names, constituting a rich tapestry. Nowhere in the world has there been such a convergence of biological, ecological, linguistic, and ethnic diversities. Nowhere in the world have the diversities been understood and explicated at the cognitive level and in various philosophical systems as in this country. The preoccupation of the Indian mind with diversities is suggested by the detailed descriptions of ecology and its features, the people, the communities, etc., in the Mahabharata, and in lexicrographical works like *Varna Ratnakar* and Abul Fazl's *Ain-i-Akbari*, among many other texts. In fact, the civilizational processes that developed in the subcontinent were also all about interaction of identities, and understanding and tolerance of diversities out of which emerged the vision of unity in diversities—now of diversities in unity. Underlining the understanding of the diversities was the feeling of unity in cultural terms and in terms of values intuitively felt by the rulers and the people. Jawaharlal Nehru defined Indianness as a matter of feeling. There was always the geographical notion of the country, as a whole, as a well-defined space, which translated into the notion of cultural unity that transcended political boundaries, and of a political unity of a large territory, or a whole of it. The colonial period saw the consolidation of this process, and the backlash of nationalism provided the emotional and ideological support for national unity.

Space and time are two dimensions of the interaction of various constituents of culture which is coterminous with society. India's diversities are accommodated within the well-defined geographi-cal region that it is, its distinct regions (thirty five), and sub-regions (ninety-one). These spaces are defined by language, territory, ecology, culture, and state systems. Each region and sub-region of India has its own cluster of communities, and its ecology explains the presence of peasants, artisans, pastoralists, tribes, fisherfolk, and so on. The time depth extends far back to the beginning of early human civilizations, and interaction between culture and identities can be seen in all phases of history, a few salient features of which may be described.

First, the study of the earliest skeletal remains suggests the pres-ence of mixed populations. Successive waves of immigration in the

pre-historic period explain the occurrence of the high biological vari-
ability among our populations. The variation in terms of morphological and genetic traits is more within a population group than between
groups. Second, the four language families have closely interacted not
only in terms of borrowing of vocabulary but also in terms of syntax,
and this is a process that is still going on. This interaction explains
the existence of the high level of bilingualism in areas where many
languages or languages of different language families meet. People
speak as many as four to five languages in such contact situations,
and the tribals generally speak three languages everywhere. All regions
of India are multilingual and multiscriptal in spite of the presence of
state/scheduled languages. Third, various identities have interacted
at the regional level. As a result of this a vibrant regional identity
has emerged. India's regions evolved during the period from second
century BC to sixteenth century AD from Tamilaham to Assam. They
are all defined by language, territory, ecology, material culture in its
multiple forms such as cuisine, dress, and so on, and culture including
multiplicity of beliefs and rituals at the local level. Above all, we find
at the regional level the intermingling of various streams—the Tantra,
the Bhakti, and the Sufi—which have left a legacy of profound human-
ism, which is a living reality. Therefore, we find at the regional level
a greater sharing of traits among communities including those who
have immigrated. Similarly, at the ethnic level we find a community
located in an ecological niche, which defines itself by endogamy, com-
mensality, hierarchy, and descent, which tries to preserve its identity
and autonomy, and which is engaged in the process of defining and
redefining its relationship with others. The communities thus placed
in a situation share a great many cultural traits across religious divide
in terms of local traditions, language/dialect, cuisine, and so on. There
are strong bonds of interdependence in matters of economy and rituals,
in politics and movements; there is a high level of participation, even
a specific role, for members of a community in other communities'
social/religious festivals and festivities. It is also appropriate here to
recall that the diversities are accommodated within hierarchies and go
with inequalities and inequities, which explain divisions and violence
in our society.

In history when cultures first confront one another, there is often a clash. But as people settle down, a process of interaction, give and take, begins, out of which emerges understanding and tolerance. Syncretism has occurred in all ages and is still an ongoing process in many regions of the country, including the tribal. It occurred on a significant scale in the medieval period, when after a phase of conflict marked by bigotry, remarkable synergy was noticed in the domain of language/ literature, technology, art and culture, and above all spirituality and human values. India's composite culture was influenced inter alia by the medieval factor. India's freedom struggle accepted the composite culture, with its elements of togetherness and rootedness as the basis of Indian nationalism. There were however voices of dissent. There still are.

Recent studies have highlighted the range, depth, and dynamism of composite culture, that is, the culture of all people of India, at all levels of identity. All regions of India are a macrocosm, a meeting ground of various streams—cultural, biological, and linguistic. All communities of India are a microcosm of many influences. All of us are legatees of many traditions, of a composite culture.

However, the legacy of composite culture should not be taken for granted. It faces real threat from the forces released by both fundamentalism and globalization. The first posits the vision of a unidimensional, homogenizing, hegemonistic, monocultural way of life to be achieved by force or by terror. The second is perceived largely in terms of a cultural counterpart of the economy of globalization which, it is feared, will destroy cultural relativism. Today, all those linkages which brought us together are under attack. Nationalism is being dismissed as a transplant. Syncretism is being described as a medieval relic. The nation state, which is a product of the anti-colonial struggle, is being considered a nuisance by multinationals which want direct access to resources. The shared cultural space is shrinking, and at stake is the survival of culture as we understand it, which has flourished in conditions of diversities, tolerance, and freedom. Therefore, the need for renewal, for a sustained struggle to preserve elements of composite culture—and its symbols—which is a priceless human legacy, and for a cultural policy that promotes it.

II

Inter-community linkages deserve to be studied as a separate subject because the study of a community is often unidimensional; there is preoccupation with the self to the neglect of the other. This can also be said about ethnicity and nationality. The ethnic perception has had its utility. Preservation of identity was and is necessary. But now we see the other consequences of the preoccupation with ethnicity: the break up of or growing threat to plural society, civil wars, violence, and disruption of all sorts. Therefore, the need for the understanding of a composite society, where it exists, and the functioning of its linkages, both traditional and modern.

The contours of our composite society are by now well known and well established: 3,000 communities, 80,000 segments and other components, 321 languages, and twenty-five scripts, all of the four morphological types, and twenty-nine genetical markers of population, all major religions and innumerable minor religions, making unity in diversity. This is a thing to be proud of as an Indian, as an *India Today* survey recently reports.

It is natural that when such identities come together or are thrown together within a space there should be suspicion, misunderstanding, even conflict and clashes. But in the long history of human culture, which is more ancient than religion, more resilient and vibrant, there is life after every clash. People settle down, start the process of interaction, integrate, and even enmesh themselves in the higher domains of literature, music, and spirituality.

Syncretism as a process of interaction has worked in all phases of history and it still works. Communities borrow from one another language, couture, cuisine, and many other things at the mundane level in day-to-day life. Immigrants seek to establish rapport with the indigenous people and come to terms with the old culture. Members of a communitiy visit sacred sites of another. There is an innate respect for the sacred. The participation level in one another's socio-religious festivals is as high as 90 per cent. Twenty per cent communities have specific roles as artisans and service castes in religious functions of other communities. A visit to a religious festival, a *puja* or an *urs* is instructive as an experience in intercommunity relationship, no matter how small or big it may be.

Through the People of India (PoI) project we tried to look at the intercommunity linkages at the level of the region or kaum which is a natural level of division in Indian history and society. Maulana Abul Kalam Azad had something most perceptive to say about identity as a kaum as pitted against religious identity. As he said, Indian Hindus and Muslims are religious adversaries—a matter that can be sorted out—but they are not rivals as a kaum; they share language, culture, and ethos of a region. But Indian Muslims going to Pakistan or Bangladesh would encounter rival kaums, such as the Pathan, Baluch, Punjabi, and the Bengali. India is a land of regions defined by ecology, language, territory, local forms of religion and culture, elements of life-cycle ceremonies, folklore, and folkculture. Each region has its own cluster of jatis, castes and communities, and their components. Each has its categories of peasants, tribes, artisans and craftsmen, fisherfolk, and so on.

It is at the regional level therefore that we can best study the diversities, heterogeneity, and rootedness of communities and inter-community linkages, including interdependence in economy and rituals, and this we did under the PoI project. Our finding was as follows:

The data set made available now suggests that people in religious categories share a high precentage of traits. Hindu–Muslim (97.7 per cent), Hindu–Buddhist (91 per cent), Hindu–Sikh (88.99 per cent) and Hindu–Jain (77.46 per cent). Other religious communities with a high percentage are Muslim–Sikh (89.95 per cent), Muslim–Buddhist (91.18 per cent) and Jain–Buddhist (81.34 per cent).

(K.S. Singh, 2002a: 112)

These traditional linkages which still exist explain how after every searing experience rehabilitation within regional communities is faster, as suggested by materials on rehabilitation. The geography of violence in the country suggests that violence is restricted to urban areas and the vast countryside is generally serene. Of course, with the rise in tension the atmosphere is vitiated, but invocation of traditional linkages and a combination of institutional support and popular mobilization may help in controlling the situation.

Modern linkages are fostered by members of the middle classes emerging across all castes and religious groups which include professionals, and political leaders. Their roles are going to be more important as the economy develops, and as globalization and resistance to globalization intensify.

The partition of the country was a setback to the composite culture. Syncretism is still under attack. The fundamenalists are trying to craft their followers in the scriptural image. They deny all links with history, economy, culture, and regional ethos. Their agents spout venom. The kaum about which the maulana spoke in the 1940s is being undermined, even communalized. Religious identities are getting consolidated, and are distancing themselves from one another. In the course of the freedom struggle we regarded composite culture, of which respect for all religions was a part, as the foundation of composite nationalism. Inter-faith dialogue should go on to promote mutual understanding. There is nothing wrong in being a devout follower of one's religion, but wider linkages between history, economy, and culture should not be ignored.

However, syncretism is alive, even vibrant, as it is a part of culture. An impressive documentation exists of syncretic traditions all over the country. In the Barak valley of Assam, a pir is worshipped along with Kali in a kalibari during puja. Sai Baba of Shirdi, looking every inch a pir and worshipped like a god by Hindus, remains the most outstanding icon of syncretism in India. In the Kashmir valley, 67 per cent of the people showed in a survey their preference to retain *kashmiriyat*, the local variant of syncretism. In Kerala, Onam—that commemorates the return of Mahabali, the good king—is celebrated by all religious communities at the regional level.

The enormous scale of interaction going on among people and communities aided by technology in the secular and even cultural sphere, despite some evidence of the withdrawal syndrome and alienation, gives ground for hope. A study in Andhra on the network of friendship shows that a very large number of people when asked to identify five of their best friends identified them outside their community.

However, there is no room for complacency, and appropiate strategies should be worked out to address issues. The elements of the strategy to restore and promote inter-community linkages should include a statement on the composite heritage in each region, the existential nature of inter-relationships which have survived periodical crises, and the tasks ahead which should include definition and celebration of our regional identity and the participation of all communities in one another's socio-religious functions, at a still higher level. Even small gestures on such occasions have a profound symbolism. People need to be told that while the identity and rights of all groups should be respected, what we have in common is more than what we do not have, and that similarities and differences are a legitimate part of an ongoing process of change and adjustment, which is to be seen in the context that also keeps changing all the time.

Community linkages in contemporary Indian society, tolerance, peaceful coexistence, and sharing of cultural and emotional spaces are not things of the past; they are still an important part of India's collective life, particularly in the rural areas. In India's rural society various communities and social groups still share material traits, social and cultural spaces, languages and dialects, local customs and festivals, kinship organizations, regional ethos and identities, whereas it is not so in urban society. And hence, there is the need for general consciousness of the society to develop more and more of inter-community interaction for better understanding of each other. During the last few decades, urban society has undergone considerable change in its perception of community life. Unfortunately, the trend has been negative, unfolding in the present scenario of communal disharmony and inter-community hostility. To cope with the existing situation, the inter-community linkages in the Indian society, particularly in urban areas, must be maintained and encouraged by all who believe in the peace and prosperity of the country. Unity in diversity and diversity in unity is not a mantra to be chanted ritually and mechanically but to be observed and absorbed in day-to-day life.

Appendix
List of Communities/Segments

1. Manda Jatiya

Nagala, Tongla (Gangol), Tapasi, Teli, Tivara, Turia (Turi), Tuluka, Turikatara, Dheola, Dhangala (Dhangar), Dhakala, Dhanuk (hillmen, archers and flowers), Dhoara, Dhuniya, Dhalikara (door-keeper), Domva (Dom), Dovatarua, Khangi (Khangar), Sagaara, Hadia, Dhadhi, Bhala, Chandaara, Chamaara, Pataniya, Parigaha, Chawi, Mundawari (Mundari-dapper or Mund barber), Vonda, Kadava, Nagara. (40)

2. *Criminal Tribes*

Lobhi, Lavala, Laptora, Nanda, Narjih, Lampaka, Chora (thief), Chanchal (cunning fellow), Juara, Chhinara (libertine), Lagavara, Petakata (pinchbellied), Naakata (with nose cleft), Kanakata (earless). (14)

3. Vanik Putran *or Trading Castes*

Sadhu, Swadhyayik, Sanuvah, Yashvahan, Babudhi, Sayeyan, Sarath, Sinhala, Malakar, Gandhavanik, Ratnaparikshak, Velavar, Vaman. (13)

4. *Castes Attending on the Ruler*
Goar, Vari, Vanik, Bauria, Kanwar (Kalwar), Mukhia, Varitha, Choragah, Agahara, Koeri, Kurmi, Rajak (or Dhobi), Nau. (13)

5. *Description of Forest* (Van Varnan) *and of Jati Dwelling in Forest* (Vantar)
Koch Kirat, Kolha, Bhil, Khas, Pulind, Savara, Chhaianga, Mlechha, Gontha, Vot, Nat, Pahalia, Podh, Donwar, Sagar, Bhatar (all described as mlechcha). (17)

6. *Hill* (Parvat) *Dwelling Communities*
Gond, Patgond, Savara, Kirata, Babbar, Bhil, Pukkam, Panchari, Medh, Mangar. (10)

7. *Description of* Rajputra Kula (Rajputra Kulvarnan)
Somavansha, Suryavansha, Doda, Chausi, Chola, Sena, Pal, Yadav, Paamaar, Nand, Nikumbha, Pushpabhuti, Shrinagar, Arhaan, Gupjharjhar, Suruki, Shikhar, Bayekwar, Gaanahwar, Survar, Meda, Mahar, Vat, Kool, Kachhawah, Vayesh, Karamba, Heyana, Chhevarak, Chhuriyoj, Bhond, Bhim, Vinha, Pundiriyan, Chauhan, Chhind, Chhikor, Chandel, Chanuki, Kanchiwala, Ranchkant, Mundaut, Vikaut, Gulahaut, Changal, Chhahela, Bhati, Mandatta, Sinhavirbhahma, Khati, Raghuvansh, Panihar, Surabhanch, Gumar, Gandhar, Vardhan, Vahhom, Vishishtha, Gutiya, Bhadra, Khursam, Vahattari. (62)

8. *Beggars* (Bhikari)
Jaga, Jogi, Nagaarika, Ratnaparikshaka, Vanitapati, Supkara, Prasadhaka, Gandhakara, manimarajna, Lipivachka, Srutidhara, Sanstrajha, Vari, Varika, Kanvara, Jaga, Yogi, Nagari, Bharahara, Bhandaua, Chatariya, Surataiya. (21)

Bibliography

1883, *Census of India, 1881: The Indian Empire Statistics of Population,* vol. 2, tables by W.C. Plowden, Kolkata: Superintendent of Government Printing.

1893, *Census of India, 1891: India General Tables for British Provinces and Feudatory States-Cases, Tribes and Races,* vol. 2, tables by J. Athelstine Bains, London: Eyre and Spottis Woode.

1903, *Census of India, 1901: India Tables,* vol. 1-A, part 2, Kolkata: Superintendent of Government Printing.

1913, *Census of India, 1911: India Tables,* vol. 1, part 2, tables, Kolkata: Superintendent of Government Printing.

1923, *Census of India, 1921: India Tables,* vol. 1, part 2, tables by J.T. Marten, Kolkata: Superintendent of Government Printing.

1931, *Census of India, 1931: India-Imperial Tables,* vol. 1, part 2, tables by J.H. Hutton, New Delhi: Manager of Publications.

1943, *Census of India, 1941: India Report and Tables,* vol.1, part 1, tables by M.W.M. Yeats, New Delhi: Manager of Publications.

Abul Fazl, Allami, 1867–77 (1927), *Ain-i-Akbari,* trans. H. Blochmann (vol. 1), H.S. Jarret (vols 2–3), Kolkata: Bibliotheca Indica (New Delhi: Manohar).

Ali, M. Athar, 1990, 'Encounter and Efflorescence', in *Proceedings of the Indian History Congress, Golden Jubilee,* Gorakhpur, pp. 1–17.

Ambedkar, B.R., 1987–90, *Dr Babasaheb Ambedkar: Writings and Speeches,* 17 vols, Mumbai: Government of Maharashtra.

Aryan, Subhashini, 1992, 'The Hidimba Devi Temple in Mandi', *Swagat*, Indian Airlines, February.

Barrier, N. Gerald, 2001, 'Sikh Identity in Historical and Contemporary Perspective', in Pashaura Singh and N. Gerald Barrier (eds), *Sikh Identity Continuity and Change*, New Delhi: Manohar.

Barua, B.K., 1951, *A Cultural History of Assam (Early Period)*, vol. 1, Guwahati: K.K. Barua, pp. 18–19.

Basu, Arbinda and J. Sreenath, 1995, *Anthropometric Variation in Assam, Bihar and Orissa*, Kolkata: Anthropological Survey of India.

_____, 1996a, *Anthropometric Variation in Maharashtra and Gujarat*, Kolkata: Anthropological Survey of India.

_____, 1996b, *Anthropometric Variations in Punjab, Haryana, Himachal Pradesh and Jammu & Kashmir*, Kolkata: Anthropological Survey of India.

Bayly, C.A., 1985, 'The Pre-history of "Communalism"? Religious Conflict in India, 1700–1860', *Modern Asian Studies*, vol. 19, no. 2, pp. 177–203.

Bhatty, Zarian, 1997, 'Social Stratification among Muslims in India', in M.N. Srinivas (ed.), *Caste: Its Twentieth Century Avatar*, New Delhi: Penguin Books.

Blunt, E.A.H., 1931, *Caste System of Northern India to the Special Reference to the United Provinces of Agra and Oudh.*

Bose, N.K., 1941, 'The Hindu Method of Tribal Absorption', *Science and Culture*, vol. 7, pp. 188–94.

Bose, N.K. (ed.), 1961, *Peasant Life in India: A Study in Indian Unity and Diversity*, memoir no. 8, Kolkata: Anthropological Survey of India.

Buchanan, Francis, 1928, *An Account of the District of Purnea in 1809–10*, Patna: Bihar and Orissa Research Society.

_____, 1939, *An Account of the District of Bhagalapur in 1810–11*, Patna: Bihar and Orissa Research Society, 1939, pp. 66–169.

_____, 1934, *An Account of the District of Shahabad in 1812–13*, Patna: Bihar and Orissa Research Society.

Chatterjee, Suniti Kumar, 1951, *Kirata Janakirti: The Indo-Mongoloids: Their Contribution to the History and Culture of India.*

Chatterjee, Suniti Kumar and Babua Mishra (eds), 1940, *Varna Ratnakara of Jyotirisvara Kavi-sekharacharya*, Bibliotheca Indica, no. 262, Kolkata: Royal Asiatic Society of Bengal.

Chaudhury, Mamata, *Tribes of Ancient India*, Kolkata: Indian Museum, 1951.

Choudhary, Radakrishan, 1970, *History of Muslim Rule in Tirhut*, Varanasi: Chowkhamba Publication.

_____, 1976, *Mithila in the Age of Vidyapati*, Varanasi: Chowkhamba Orientalia.

Crooke, William, 1974 (1896), *The Tribes and Castes of North Western India*, vol. 1 Delhi: Cosmo Publications.

_____, 1896, *The Tribes and Castes of the North West Provinces and Oudh*, Superintendent of Government Printing.

Dalton, E.T., 1872, *Descriptive Ethnology of Bengal*, Calcutta: Office of the Superintendent of Government Press.

Desai, G.H., 1912, *A Glossary of Castes, Tribes and Races in Baroda State*, Mumbai.

Diddamari, Mohammad Azam, AH 1303, *Tarikh-i-Azami*, Muhammadi Press, Lahore; Urdu translation under *Tarikh-i-Kashmir Azami* by Munshi Ashraf Ali, Delhi Madrassa, Delhi 1846.

Dube, S.C., 1951, *The Kamar*, Lucknow: The Universal Publishers Ltd.

Duggal, K.S., 1997, 'Indo-Pak Dialogue: Building Bridges of Understanding', *Mainstream*, vol. 1, November, pp. 7–9.

Elwin, Verrier, 1945, 'Comments', *Man in India*, vol. 25, no. 1, March.

Endle, Sindney, *The Kacharis*, London: Macmillan & Co., 1911, pp. 6–7.

Enthoven, R.E., 1975 (1920), *The Tribes and Castes of Bombay*, 3 vols, New Delhi: Cosmo Publications.

Fouq, Munshi Mohammad Din, 1934, *Tarikh-i-Aqwam-i-Kashmir*, Lahore (in Urdu).

Ghosh, G.C., 1988, *All India Bio-Anthropological Survey: Preliminary Tables*, Anthropological Survey of India.

Gopal, S., 1986, 'Nehru, Religion and Secularism', in R. Champakalakshmi and S. Gopal (eds), *Tradition, Dissent and Ideology: Essays in Honour of Romila Thapar*, New Delhi: Oxford University Press, 1986, pp. 195–215.

Government of India, 1975, *Amir Khusrau: A Memorial Volume*, New Delhi: Publications Division, Ministry of Information and Broadcasting, 1975.

_____, 2002, *National Human Development Report, 2001*, Planning Commission, Government of India, Oxford, March.

Griffiths, Walter G., 1946, *The Kol Tribe of Central India*, Calcutta: The Royal Asiatic Society of Bengal.

Guha, B.S., 1933, 'Racial Affinities of the Peoples of India', in *Census if India 1931*, vol. 3, Simla: Government of India Press.

Guha, Ramachandra, *Savaging the Civilized: Verrier Elwin,His Tribals, and India*, New Delhi: Oxford University Press, 1999.

Habib, Irfan, 'The Formation of India: Notes of the History of an Idea', *Social Scientist*, Jul–Aug 1997, vol. 25, nos 7–8, pp. 3–10.

Hasan, Siraj-ul, 1923, *Castes and Tribes of H.E.H., The Nizam's Dominions*, Government of Hyderabad, Hyderabad.

Hershman, Paul, 1981, *Punjabi Kinship and Marriage*, ed. Hilary Standing, Delhi: Hindustan Publishing Corporation.

Hunter, W.W., 1877, *A Statistical Account of Bengal*, vol. 19, London: Trubner & Co.

Ibbetson, Denzil, 1883, *Punjab Castes*, Lahore: Superintendent of Government Printing, 1883.

Indira Gandhi Memorial Trust, 2003, *Architecture of an Inclusive Society*, New Delhi: Mudrit Publishers.

Iyer, L.K.A., 1935, *The Travancore Tribes and Castes*, vol. 2, Thiruvananthapuram: Government Press.

Jahangir, 1910–14, *Tuzuk-i-Jahangiri*, 2 vols., trans. A. Rogers and H. Beveridge, London.

Jha, D.N. (ed.), 1995, Society and Ideology in India: Essays in Honour of Professor R.S. Sharma, New Delhi: Munshiram Manoharlal.

Jha, Hetukar (ed.), 2002, *Perspectives on Indian Society: A Critique*, New Delhi: Manohar.

Jumsai, Sumet, 1997, *Naga: Cultural Origins and the West Pacific*, Bangkok: Chalermnet Press and D.D. Books.

Kabui, Gangmumei, 2003, *History of Manipur: Pre-colonial Period, Volume 1*, New Delhi: National Publishing House.

Karve, Irawati, 1974, *Yuganta: End of an Epoch*, Sangam Book.

Kosambi, D.D., 2009, *The Oxford India Kosambi: Combined Methods in Indology and Other Writings*, ed. Brajadulal Chattopadhyaya, New Delhi: Oxford University Press, 2009.

Krishan, S. (ed.), *Linguistic Traits across Language Boundaries: A Report on All India Linguistic Traits Survey*, Kolkata: Anthropological Survey of India, 1990.

Kulke, Hermann, 1976, 'Kshatriyaization and Social Change in Post Medieval Orissa', S. Debas Pillai (ed.), *Changing India, Study in Honor of Cohuryo*, Bombay: Popular Prakashan, pp. 398–409.

_____, 1978, 'Jagannatha as the State Deity under the Gajapatis of Orissa' in A. Eschmaan *et al.*, *The Cult of Jagannath and the Regional Tradition of Orissa*, New Delhi: Manohar.

Kulke, Hermann, 1979, 'Early State Formation and Royal Legitimation in Tribal Areas of Eastern India', in R. Moser and M.K. Gautam (eds), Aspects of Tribal Life in South Asia, Bern: Studio Ethnological Bemensia.

Kulke, Hermann, and Dietmar Rothermund, 1990, A History of India, New York: Dorset Press.

Leuva, K.K., 1963, The Asur: A Study of Primitive Iron-smelters, Bharatiya Adimjati Sevak Sangh, New Delhi.

Madan, T.N., 1998, 'Composite Culture: Inadequacies of Secular Response', Times of India, 4 April.

Majumdar, Biman Bihari, 1983, 'Vidyapati and His Age', in S.H. Askari and Qeyamuddin Ahmad (eds), Comprehensive History of Bihar, vol. II, part I, Appendix II, Patna: K.P. Jayaswal Research Institute, pp. 366–95.

Majumder, Partha P., B. Uma Shankar, Amitabha Basu, Kailash C. Malhotra, Ranjan Gupta, Barun Mukhopadhyay, M. Vijayakumar, and Subrata K. Roy, 1982, 'Distribution of ANBO Blood Groups on the Indian Subcontinent: A Cluster Analytic Approach', Current Anthropology, vol. XXIII, no. 5, pp. 539–66.

_____, 'Anthropometric Variation in India: A Statistical Appraisal', Current anthropology, vol. XXXI, no. 1, 1990, pp. 94–103.

Malik, Aditya, 1994, 'Violence, Death and Marriage in the Oral Epic of Devnarayan', paper presented at the national seminar on Rajasthan, Jaipur, 14–18 December.

Malik, Z.U., 1990, 'The Core and the Periphery: A Contribution to the Debate on the Eighteenth Century', Proceedings of the Indian History Congress, 51st session, Kolkata, 1990, pp. 169–99.

Mazumdar, B.C., 1927, The Aborigins of the Highlands of Central India, Calcutta: University of Calcutta.

Mehta, B.M., 1984, The Gonds of the Central Indian High lands, New Delhi: Concept Publishing Company.

Mishra, K.C., 1987, Tribes in the Mahabharata: A Socio-cultural Study, New Delhi: National Publishing House.

Momin, A.R., 1998, 'Composite Culture Is Not Just Skin-deep', Times of India, 25 April.

Narain, A.K., 1957 (1980), The Indo-Greeks, Delhi: Oxford University Press.

Nesfield, John C., 1885, A Brief Views of the Castes System of the North Western Provinces and Oudh, Allahabad, North Western Provinces and Oudh Government Press, 1885.

Padmanabha, P., 1983, *Indian Census and Anthropological Investigations*, Delhi: Controller of Publications.

Pandas, S.C., 1986, *Naga Cult in Orissa*, Delhi: B.R. Publishing Corporation.

Panigrahi, K.C., 1986, *History of Orissa*, Cuttack: Kitab Mahal.

Parasher Sen, 1991, Aloka, *Mlecchas in Early India*, New Delhi: Munshiram Manoharlal.

Radhakrishnan, S., 2004, 'Mahavira and His Religion', in *Indian Religion*, reprinted in *Cultural and Religious Heritage of India: Jainism*, ed. Usha Sharma, New Delhi: Mittal Publication.

_____, 1915 (1969), *The People of India*, Kolkata: Thacker & Spinck (New Delhi: Oriental Books).

Risley, H.H., 1891 (1981), *The Tribes and Castes of Bengal*, 2 vols, Kolkata: Bengal Secretariat Press, 1891 (reprint Kolkata: Firma Mukhopadhaya, 1981).

Rose, H.A., 1919, *Glossary of the Tribes and Castes of the Punjab and North-west Frontier Province*, vol. 2, Lahore: Civil and Military Gazette Press.

Russell, R.V. and Hiralal, Rai Bahadur, 1918 (1975), *The Tribes and Castes of the Central Provinces of India*, vols 1–4, London, New Delhi: Cosmo Publications.

Saksena, Rashmi, 1994, 'Faithfully Yours: A Unique Relationship Binds Hindus and Muslims of 60 Villages of Uttar Pradesh', *The Week*, 13 February.

Sen, Geeti, 2003, 'Visions: Scripting the Nation', *IIC Quarterly*, vol. 29, Winter 2002–Spring 2003, pp. 2–12.

Sen, Geeti, and Ashis Banerjee, 2001, *The Human Landscape*, New Delhi: Orient Longman and India International Centre.

Shafer, Robert, 1954, *Ethnography of Ancient India*, Weisbaden: Otto Harrassowitz.

Shastri, Ajay Mitra (ed.), 2004, Mahabharata: The End of an Era (Yuganta), New Delhi: Aryan Books International.

Sherwani, H.K. and P.M. Joshi (eds), 1973, *History of Medieval Deccan*, vol. 1, Hyderabad: Government of Andhra Pradesh, 1973.

Shrimali, Krishna Mohan, 1998, 'Cultural Nationalism Saps Culture, Nation', *Times of India*, 26 May.

_____, 1993, *Hindu–Muslim Relations*, Kolkata: Adadi Publications.

Siddiqui, M.K.A., 1979, 'Islamization among the Tribes of Central and Western India', *Bulletin of the Anthropological Survey of India*, vol. 35, nos 3–4, July–September.

Singh, Chetan, 2000, 'Interpreting Territory: Shifting Identities and the Problem of Defining the Region', presented at the national seminar on

'The Challenge of States: Democracy, Ethnicity and Governance', mimeo, Bhopal, 13–15 December.

Singh, Khushwant, 1998, 'See on TV', *Hindustan Times,* 21 March 1998.

Singh, K.S., 1985, *Tribal Society of India: An Anthropo-historical Perspective*, New Delhi: Manohar Publications, 1985.

_____, 1988, 'Famine Nationalism and Social Change: The Indian Scenario', *Indian Historical Review,* vol. 14, nos 1–2, pp. 186–205.

Singh, K.S., 1992, *People of India: An Introduction*, Calcutta: Anthropological Survey of India.

_____, 1993, *Material Trail Survey: Additional Data Basketry in India,* Kolkata: Anthropological Survey of India.

_____, 1994a, 'Towards a Documentary History of Anthropological Survey of India', mimeo, New Delhi: Anthropological Survey of India.

_____, 1994b, 'The People of India: Making of a National Project', mimeo, New Delhi: Anthropological Survey of India.

_____, 1996a, 'Reflections on Historical Ethnography in India', in C.P. Singh (ed.), *Studies in Indian History and Culture*, vol. 3, Patna: K.P. Jaiswal Research Institute, pp. 1–9.

_____, 1996b, 'Census and Ethnography', in S.P. Mohanty and A.R. Menon (eds), *Census as Social Document*, Jaipur and New Delhi: Rawat Publications, pp. 138–46.

_____, 1997a, 'People of India, Diversities and Linkages', in *The Indian Experience,* Indian Airlines, 1997.

_____, 1997b, 'Varna Ratnakar and Its Ethnography,' mimeo, 1997.

_____, 1997c, 'Towards a Documentary History of Anthropological Survey of India', mimeo, vol. 2, New Delhi: Anthropological Survey of India, New Delhi, 1997.

_____, 1997d, 'The Emerging Tribal Scenario', *IIC Quarterly*, Spring, pp. 85–91.

_____, 1997e, 'The People of India, Diversities and Linkages', in *The Indian Experience*, Media Transasia Limited, 1997, pp. 34–43.

_____, 1998a, 'The People of India: Diversities and Linkages', in D. Balasubrahmanian and N. Appaji Rao (eds), *The Indian Human Heritage*, Hyderabad: Universities Press.

_____, 1998b, 'Diversity, Heterogenety, Integration: An Ideological Perspective', in S. Setter and P.K.V. Kaemal (eds), *We Lived Together*, New Delhi: Pragati Publications and Indian Council of Historical Research, pp. 233–49.

_____, 2000a, 'The Ethnography of the Mahabharata and the North-East', mimeo.

Singh, K.S., 2000b, 'A Perspective on Anthropological Survey of India', *Seminar*, no. 495, November, pp. 40–4.

_____, 2000c, 'Tribal Customary Laws Policy Implication', *Yojana*, vol. 44, no. 8, April, pp. 18–21.

_____, 2002a, 'Tribal Women: Resurrection', in Aparna Basu and Anup Taneja (eds), *Breaking out of Invisibility: Women in Indian History*, Indian Council of Historical Research, New Delhi: Northern Book Centre, 2002, pp. 206–31.

_____, (ed.), 1972, *Tribal Situation in India*, Indian Institute of Advanced Studies, 1977.

_____, (ed.), 1993a, *The Mahabharata in Tribal and Folk Traditions of India*, Shimla: Indian Institute of Advanced Study and Anthropological Survey of India, 1993.

_____, (ed.), 1993b, *Tribal Ethnography, Customary Law and Change*, Concept Publisher & Co.

_____, (ed.), 1996a, *People of India: India's Communities (A–G)*, vol. 4, New Delhi: Anthropological Survey of India.

_____, (ed.), 1996b, *People of India: Identity, Ecology, Social Organisation, Economy, Linkages and Development Processes: A Quantitative Profile*, vol. 7, New Delhi: Anthropological Survey of India.

_____, (ed.), 1996c, *People of India: Communities, Segments, Synonyms, Surnames and Titles*, vol. 8, New Delhi: Anthropological Survey of India.

_____, (ed.), 1998a, *People of India: India's Communities (H–M)*, vol. 5, New Delhi: Anthropological Survey of India.

_____, (ed.), 1998b, *People of India: India's Communities (N–Z)*, vol. 6, New Delhi: Anthropological Survey of India.

_____, 2002b, 'Varna Ratnakar and Its Ethnography', in HetukarJha (ed.), *Perspectives on Indian Society and History: A Critique*, New Delhi: Manohar Publications, pp. 109–21.

Sinha, B.K., 1998, 'The Answers Within', *Down to Earth*, 11 May.

Sircar, D.C., 1967, *Cosmography and Geography in Early Indian Literature*, Indian Studies: Past and Present, Kolkata: D. Chattopadhyaya.

Thapar, Romila, 1996, 'The Tyranny of Labels', *Social Scientist*, vol. 24, nos 9–10, September–October, pp. 3–23.

Thurston, E., 1987, *Castes and Tribes of Southern India*, 7 vols, New Delhi: Cosmo Publications.

Tod, James, 1829, 'Annals and Antiquities of Rajasthan or The Central and Western Rajput States of India'.

Index

685671S

11:4